WHY READ AND STUDY GENESIS?

In Genesis, its first book, the Bible hits the ground running and shows us the kind of people we could see today on the news, or meet on the street, wrestling with God to find happiness, success, and love in a world gone wrong. They struggle. They suffer. They do right, and they do wrong. With God's help, sometimes they fight their way through to a happy ending. And God builds on the struggles, the suffering, and the good and bad choices to start making a way for anyone in the world to find their way back to him.

Maybe you've never read the book of Genesis. Or maybe you've tried but never got past the opening because of arguments you've heard about Adam and Eve and evolution. You owe it to yourself to take another look. From a perspective deeply immersed in real human life, Genesis gives us the big picture of what kind of world God wants this to be, how it became something else instead, and what God has been doing ever since, by meeting people just where they are, to make things right again.

The main purpose of Genesis is to explain how one family and its descendants came to have a special role in God's plans for all of humanity. The book first shows God creating a world of order and harmony. This order and harmony is shattered when people turn away from God. The world is filled with violence and injustice that God has to take extreme measures to restrain. But then God begins to restore the beautiful world he'd designed by entering into a relationship with one person who trusts and believes in him in a special way: Abraham. God extends this relationship down through the generations of Abraham's descendants. Eventually they grow into a tribe that *could* become the beginning of a restored human community—if they could just live up to God's friendship and favor.

This study guide will take you through Genesis story by story and character by character. You won't see Noah in a bathrobe collecting cuddly animals for the ark. You won't be asked to debate the age of the earth. But you will meet people just like you being disappointed and betrayed and rescued and blessed as the world God sets in motion goes careening off into the future without any brakes. Fasten your seat belt.

UNDERSTANDING THE
BOOKS OF THE BIBLE

GENESIS

Also available in the
UNDERSTANDING THE BOOKS OF THE BIBLE series:

John
Wisdom: Proverbs/Ecclesiastes/James—October 2010
Biblical Apocalypses: Daniel/Revelation—October 2010

Future releases:

Exodus/Leviticus/Numbers
New Covenants: Deuteronomy/Hebrews
Joshua/Judges/Ruth
Samuel–Kings

Amos/Hosea/Micah/Isaiah
Zephaniah/Nahum/Habakkuk/Jeremiah/Obadiah
Ezekiel/Haggai/Zechariah/Jonah/Joel/Malachi

Psalms/Song of Songs/Lamentations
Job
Chronicles/Ezra/Nehemiah/Esther

Matthew
Mark
Luke–Acts

Thessalonians/Corinthians/Galatians/Romans
Colossians/Ephesians/Philemon/Philippians/Timothy/Titus
Peter/Jude/John

UNDERSTANDING THE BOOKS OF THE BIBLE

GENESIS

Christopher R. Smith

Biblica Publishing
We welcome your questions and comments.

USA   1820 Jet Stream Drive, Colorado Springs, CO 80921
India   Logos Bhavan, Medchal Road, Jeedimetla Village, Secunderabad 500 055, A.P.

UNDERSTANDING THE BOOKS OF THE BIBLE: Genesis
ISBN-13: 978-1-60657-055-5

12 11 10 / 6 5 4 3 2 1

Published in 2010 by Biblica

A catalog record for this book is available through the Library of Congress.

Printed in the United States of America

CONTENTS

HOW THESE STUDY GUIDES ARE DIFFERENT

Did you know you could read and study the Bible without using any chapters or verses? The books of the Bible are real "books," and they're meant to be experienced the same way other books are: as exciting, interesting works that keep you turning pages right to the end and then make you want to go back and savor each part. The UNDERSTANDING THE BOOKS OF THE BIBLE series of study guides will help you do that with the Bible.

While you can use these study guides with any version or translation, they're especially designed to be used with *The Books of The Bible*, an edition of the Scriptures from Biblica that takes out the chapter and verse numbers and presents the biblical books in their natural form. Here's what people are saying about reading the Bible this way:

I love it. I find myself understanding Scripture in a new way, with a fresh lens, and I feel spiritually refreshed as a result. I learn much more through stories being told, and with this new format, I feel the truth of the story come alive for me.

Reading Scripture this way flows beautifully. I don't miss the chapter and verse numbers. I like them gone. They got in the way.

I've been a reader of the Bible all of my life. But after reading just a few pages without chapters and verses, I was amazed at what I'd been missing all these years.

For more information about *The Books of The Bible* or to obtain a low-cost copy, visit http://www.thebooksofthebible.info. Premium editions of this Bible will be available in Spring 2011 from Zondervan at your favorite Christian retailer.

For people who are used to chapters and verses, reading and studying the Bible without them may take a little getting used to. It's like when you get a new cell phone or upgrade the operating system on your computer. You have to unlearn some old ways of doing things and learn some new ones. But it's not too long until you catch on to how the new system works and you find you can do a lot of things you couldn't do before.

Here are some of the ways you and your group will have a better experience of the Scriptures by using these study guides.

YOU'LL FOLLOW THE NATURAL FLOW OF BIBLICAL BOOKS

This guide will take you through the book of Genesis following its natural flow. (The way the book unfolds is illustrated on page 11.) You won't go chapter-by-chapter through Genesis, because chapter divisions often come at the wrong places and break up the flow. Did you know that the chapter divisions used in most modern Bibles were added more than a thousand years after the biblical books were written? And that the verse numbers were added more than three centuries after that? If you grew up with the chapter-and-verse system, it may feel like part of the inspired Word of God. But it's not. Those little numbers aren't holy, and when you read and study Genesis without them, you'll hear the story emerge as never before.

To help you get a feel for where you are in the book's natural flow, each study session will be headed by a visual cue, like this:

Genesis > Account of Terah > Abraham Story, Episodes 1 and 2

YOU'LL UNDERSTAND WHOLE BOOKS

Imagine going to a friend's house to watch a movie you've never seen before. After only a couple of scenes, your friend stops the film and says, "So, tell me what you think of it so far." When you give your best shot at a reply, based on the little you've seen, your friend says, "You know, there's a scene in another movie that always makes me think of this one." He switches to a different movie and before you know it, you're watching a scene from the middle of another film.

Who would ever try to watch a movie this way? Yet many Bible studies take this approach to the Bible. They have you read a few paragraphs from one book of the Bible, then jump to a passage in another book. The UNDERSTANDING THE BOOKS OF THE BIBLE series doesn't do that. Instead, these study guides focus on understanding the message and meaning of one book.

Your group will read through the entire book of Genesis, not just selected chapters or verses. The thirty studies in this guide are organized into four units of six to nine studies each, so that groups that meet weekly can work through each unit in a couple of months and take a break in between if they wish.

YOU'LL DECIDE FOR YOURSELVES WHAT TO DISCUSS

In each session of this study guide there are many options for discussion. While each session could be completed by a group in about an hour and a half, any one of the questions could lead to an involved conversation. There's no need to cut the conversation short to try to "get through it all." As a group leader, you can read through all the questions ahead of time and decide which one(s) to begin with, and what order to take them up in. If you do get into an involved discussion of one question, you can leave out some of the others, or you can extend the study over more than one meeting if you do want to cover all of them.

TOGETHER, YOU'LL TELL THE STORY

Each session gives creative suggestions for reading the passage you'll be discussing. The guide will often invite the group to dramatize the Scriptures by reading them out loud like a play. The discussion options may also invite group members to retell the biblical story from a fresh perspective. This kind of telling and retelling is a spiritual discipline, similar to Bible memorization, that allows people to personalize the Scriptures and take them to heart. Our culture increasingly appreciates the value and authority of story, so this is a great discipline for us to cultivate. (If you're using *The Books of The Bible*, you'll find that the natural sections it marks off by white space correspond with the sections of the reading. If you're using another edition, you'll be able to identify these sections easily because they're identified in this guide by their opening lines.)

EVERYBODY WILL PARTICIPATE

There's plenty of opportunity for everyone in the group to participate. Because Genesis is a story with characters, as you read from it in each session you'll often have different group members taking the parts of different characters. Group members can also read the session introduction aloud or the discussion questions. As a leader, you can easily involve quiet people by giving them these opportunities. And everyone will feel that they can speak up and answer the questions, because the questions aren't looking for "right answers." Instead, they invite the group to work together to understand the Bible.

YOU'LL ALL SHARE DEEPLY

The discussion questions will invite you to share deeply about your ideas and experiences. The answers to these questions can't be found just by "looking them up." They require reflection on the meaning of the whole passage, in the wider context of Genesis, in light of your personal experience. These aren't the kinds of abstract, academic questions that make the discussion feel like a test. Instead, they'll connect the Bible passage to your life in practical, personal, relational ways.

To create a climate of trust where this kind of deep sharing is encouraged, here are a couple of ground rules that your group should agree to at its first meeting:

- *Confidentiality.* Group members agree to keep what is shared in the group strictly confidential. "What's said in the group stays in the group."
- *Respect.* Group members will treat other members with respect at all times, even when disagreeing over ideas.

HOW TO LEAD GROUP STUDIES USING THIS GUIDE

Each session has three basic parts:

Introduction to the Study

Have a member of your group read the introduction to the session out loud to everyone. Then give group members the chance to ask questions about the introduction and offer their own thoughts and examples.

Reading from Genesis

Read the selection out loud together. (The study guide will offer suggestions for various ways you can do this for each session. For example, sometimes you will assign different characters in the story to different readers, and sometimes different people will read different sections of the passage.)

Discussion Questions

Most questions are introduced with some observations. These may give some background to Jewish culture, or explain where you are in the flow of the story. After the observations there are suggested discussion questions. Many of them have multiple parts that are really just different ways of getting at an issue.

You don't have to discuss the questions in the order they appear in the study guide. You can choose to spend your time exploring just two or three questions and not do the others. Or you can have a shorter discussion of each question so that you do cover all of them. As the group leader, before the meeting you should read the questions and the observations that introduce them, and decide which ones you want to emphasize.

When you get to a given question, have someone read aloud the observations and the question. As you answer the question, interact with the observations (you can agree or disagree with them) and with the reading from Genesis. Use only part of the question to get at the issue from one angle, or use all of the parts, as you choose.

Sometimes there will be things to do or think about in preparation for your next session. But there's never any "homework" in the traditional sense.

TIPS FOR HOME GROUPS, SUNDAY SCHOOL CLASSES, COMMUNITY BIBLE EXPERIENCES, AND INDIVIDUAL USE

If you're using this guide in a *home group*, you may want to begin each meeting (or at least some meetings) by having dinner together. You may also want to have a time of singing and prayer before or after the study.

If you're using this guide in a *Sunday school class*, you may want to have a time of singing and prayer before or after the study.

This study guide can also be used in connection with a *community Bible experience* of Genesis. If you're using it in this way:

- Encourage people to read each session's Scripture passage by themselves early in the week.
- Do each session in midweek small groups.
- Invite people to write/create some response to each small-group session that could be shared in worship that weekend. These might involve poetry, journal or blog entries, artwork, dramas, videos, and so on.
- During the weekend worship services, let people share these responses, and have preaching on the Scripture passage that was studied that week. Preachers can gather up comments they've heard from people and draw on their own reflections to sum up the church's experience of that passage.

This guide can also be used for *individual study*. You can write out your responses to the questions in a notebook or journal. (However, we really encourage reading and studying the Bible in community!)

EXPERIENCING THE BOOK OF GENESIS AS A WHOLE

Before considering the individual parts of any creative work, it's important to experience it as a whole. This gives you the "big picture," the overall message, and allows you to understand each part in its proper context. Everyone in your group should read or listen to the entire book of Genesis, all at once or in just a few installments, before you do the other studies in this guide together.

If you have a copy of *The Books of The Bible,* begin by reading the introduction to Genesis in that volume. If you don't, the material on "Why Read and Study Genesis?" at the beginning of this study guide will give you a basic sense of what the book's major themes are. The outline on page 11 and the introductions to sessions 2 and 3 will show you how it's put together.

There are a number of enjoyable and meaningful ways you can read or listen to the book of Genesis:

Hold a Longer Meeting to Read Aloud. You can gather your whole group for a special longer meeting where you'll read the book of Genesis out loud. If you're doing a church-wide experience of Genesis, the entire church can gather for this activity.

The book of Genesis takes about four hours to read. You may want to begin in the early afternoon with the stories of the early history of the human race, which are covered by Unit I in this guide. Take a break for a physical activity and some informal discussion of what you've heard. Then read the stories of Abraham, Isaac and Jacob (covered in Units II and III). Take another break and have dinner together. Then finish the book in the early evening by reading the story of Joseph and his brothers (Unit IV).

For the reading itself, volunteers can take turns reading aloud from Genesis. Change readers every time you come to what seems like the end of a scene.

Listen to an Audiobook of Genesis. Alternatively, you can listen to a professional recording. You may prefer to listen to Genesis in Today's New International Version (TNIV), since that's the translation used in *The Books of The Bible* and in these studies. The *TNIV Audio Bible* by Zondervan (ISBN: 9780310922858) is available through Christian bookstores and many online outlets. The book of Genesis in the TNIV is available for free download in audio format at www.biblica.com/bible/audio/tniv/index.php.

Combine Reading and Service. Group members can also experience the whole book of Genesis together in smaller gatherings centered around fellowship, learning, and service. A few people could get together to bake homemade bread, for themselves or for a local soup kitchen. One person could teach breadmaking to the others, and everyone could read Genesis aloud while the bread is rising and baking. Another group might gather to repair small appliances for people in need and listen to a recording of the book while they work together. You can take many similar approaches, based on the interests and abilities of the people in your group, to make your experience of the whole book an occasion for community-building and service.

Reading Alone and Interacting in Social Media. People could read Genesis individually, over a defined period of time, and commit to posting online about what they're reading and to interacting with what others are saying.

Take whatever creative approach will allow you to experience the whole book in a fresh, enjoyable and meaningful way before you do the other sessions in this guide.

In whatever way you hear Genesis read out loud, as you listen to the book, the following outline can help you see how the story is unfolding.

OUTLINE OF THE BOOK OF GENESIS

The book of Genesis tells the story of humanity's earliest relationship with God. It traces the descendants of key figures to show how that relationship developed. The book alternates its focus between the community that God entered into a covenant relationship with and humanity outside that community. ("Account" means the story of a figure's descendants.)

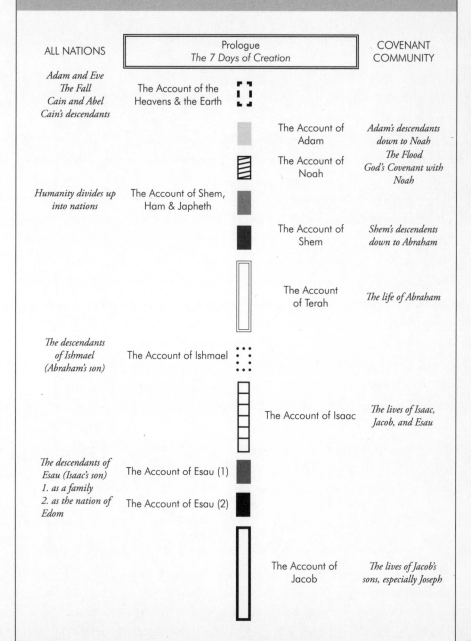

ALL NATIONS		COVENANT COMMUNITY
	Prologue *The 7 Days of Creation*	
Adam and Eve *The Fall* *Cain and Abel* *Cain's descendants*	The Account of the Heavens & the Earth	
	The Account of Adam	*Adam's descendants down to Noah*
	The Account of Noah	*The Flood* *God's Covenant with Noah*
Humanity divides up into nations	The Account of Shem, Ham & Japheth	
	The Account of Shem	*Shem's descendents down to Abraham*
	The Account of Terah	*The life of Abraham*
The descendants of Ishmael (Abraham's son)	The Account of Ishmael	
	The Account of Isaac	*The lives of Isaac, Jacob, and Esau*
The descendants of Esau (Isaac's son) *1. as a family* *2. as the nation of Edom*	The Account of Esau (1) The Account of Esau (2)	
	The Account of Jacob	*The lives of Jacob's sons, especially Joseph*

IN THE BEGINNING

THE SEVEN DAYS OF CREATION

INTRODUCTION

A magnificent lyrical prologue sets the stage for the events in the book of Genesis by depicting the kind of world that God originally established and will be working to restore.

Most of the discussion (debate, actually) about the opening of Genesis swirls around the question of how its depiction of a seven-day creation can be reconciled with modern scientific descriptions of a universe that's billions of years old. This is a very heated and complicated debate. It's not in keeping with the purposes of this study guide series to try to address or resolve it. The goal of this session will be simply to explore the text of the Genesis prologue on a literary level, to discover its internal principles and draw practical implications. So give the members of your group a moment to state their positions on the age of the universe, if they wish, and then agree to leave your positions "at the door" and not debate them with one another.

READING

Have four people read the Genesis prologue. Assign a letter from A to D to each person and have them read the parts below identified by that letter:

A: Introduction ("In the beginning . . .")

B: Day 1 ("And God said, 'Let there be light . . .'")

C: Day 2 ("And God said, 'Let there be a vault . . .'")

D: Day 3 ("And God said, 'Let the water under the sky . . .'")

B: Day 4 ("And God said, 'Let the lights . . .'")

C: Day 5 ("And God said, 'Let the water teem. . .'"):

D: Day 6 ("And God said, 'Let the land produce . . .'"):

A: Day 7 ("Thus the heavens and the earth were completed . . . because on it he rested from all the work of creating that he had done.")

DISCUSSION

1 At the beginning of the Genesis prologue, the earth isn't fulfilling God's intentions. For one thing, it's "formless." There are no boundaries within the created world that define realms of space and time where activities can properly take place. (The word translated "formless" here is used in other parts of the Bible to describe deserts where there are no roads, trails, or landmarks.) But the earth is also "empty." There are no creatures to populate, and more importantly to govern, any realms.

The prologue describes how God makes the world conform to his intentions. God first creates boundaries that divide off and define various realms, and God then populates each realm. This accomplished, God pauses to admire his creation. (The picture of the created world in Genesis, of a flat earth under a solid sky, doesn't match our modern cosmology. But it does reflect what things look like to an earthbound observer. If we accept that the Bible is speaking from an observational perspective, we can step across the cultural distance and see how God's moral and spiritual ideals for the created world are being expressed.)

Realms Created	Realms Populated	Rest
Day 1: Day, night	Day 4: Sun, moon & stars	
Day 2: Sea, sky	Day 5: Sea creatures, birds	Day 7: The Sabbath
Day 3: Land	Day 6: People, animals	

⮕ If the Genesis prologue is expressing God's ideal for creation, does this mean that our own individual and community lives should be organized into spaces and times devoted to specific purposes? How can people put boundaries in place to organize their lives? What activity would you most want to make space and time for if you could?

⮕ Where in the text do we see that the boundaries between defined spaces and times can be flexible and variable? (Think, for example, of day and night, or sea and land.) Is there any room for "creative chaos" (unstructured down time) in the life of someone who wants to pursue God's ideals? (Is this part of what's happening on the Sabbath, when God seems to have nothing planned?)

⮕ The assumption in the prologue seems to be that there's no such thing as an ungoverned space. Each realm has some "great" creature that rules it. Who or what rules the spaces and times in your life? Are there any rulers you'd like to replace with better ones?

2 In this prologue, God doesn't carry out his will by performing acts of overwhelming power. Instead, he speaks authoritative words that are obeyed. The Genesis prologue may be understood as a "royal chronicle" that records the orders of a ruler, describes how they were carried out, and notes that the ruler approved of how this was done. (The recurring formula is, "God said . . . and it was so . . . God saw that it was good.")

➲ It's been said that the "reign of God" is present on earth "wherever and whenever God's will is done without interference." This happens here at the beginning of creation. Where else do you see it happening in the world today, and in your own life? Where would you most like to see God's will done with less interference?

THE CREATION AND FALL OF HUMANITY

Book of Genesis > Account of the Heavens and the Earth > Story of Adam and Eve

INTRODUCTION

As the outline on page 11 shows, the book of Genesis has twelve major sections. Each section provides the "account" of a given person (such as Noah or Jacob). The word translated "account" comes from a Hebrew verb that means "to have offspring." The "account" of a given person is a description of what they brought into the world and how this affected humanity's relationship with God.

In Genesis, key people set events in motion that determine the course of a whole period of history. They bring characters onto the world stage who influence many others, for good or for harm. The "account" of a person is, in effect, their *legacy*.

The first "account" in Genesis speaks of "the heavens and the earth" as this kind of ancestor figure. The narrative in this part of Genesis describes what the created order first "brought forth" once it had been set in place.

In this account, the events of earliest human history are retold from a perspective that complements the one in the prologue. As in the case of the prologue, there has been much debate about how the events recounted here relate to scientific descriptions of human origins. Once again, it's not the goal of these studies to address this kind of debate. It may be helpful for group members simply to state how they understand the story of Adam and Eve: Is it literal? Symbolic? Allegorical? Something else? Each person should hold their own views on this question confidently and humbly, and join the others in engaging Genesis together on a literary level for a profitable discussion.

READING

Read the story of the creation and fall of humanity out loud in your group. (It begins, "This is the account of the heavens and the earth . . ." It runs for several pages and ends with God banishing Adam and Eve from the Garden of Eden: ". . . he placed on the east side of the Garden of Eden cherubim and a flaming sword flashing back and forth to guard the way to the tree of life.")

Have members take turns reading a paragraph at a time.

DISCUSSION

1 This account in Genesis shows how the fall of humanity resulted in broken relationships between people and creation; between one person and another; and between humanity and God.

For example, before the fall, fruit was just fruit. It was beautiful and delicious, and could be appreciated just for that. But when humans fell away from God, they began to expect created objects to do more for them than they really could: The woman decided the fruit was "good for food and pleasing to the eye, *and also desirable for gaining wisdom*" (italics added). So humanity's relationship with creation became disordered.

To give another example, before the fall, the man and woman were "allies" with a common purpose. But after the fall, the man turned against the woman and blamed her for their common decision.

⊃ What would it have been like to live in the Garden of Eden? How would it have been different from life as we know it today, particularly in terms of how we relate to creation, other people, and God?

2 Throughout the prologue, God declares various created things "good." But now God finds something that's "not good." It's not good for the man to be alone. He needs a "helper." This Hebrew term doesn't refer to an "assistant." In the rest of the Old Testament, it describes a strong ally. (The term is used most often of God, as in Psalm 121: "My *help* comes from the LORD, the Maker of heaven and earth," italics added.) The ally who's needed here is literally a "counterpart" to the man. The complementary beings in this partnership will be stronger, safer, and more capable together than either one would be alone.

⮑ What are some of the significant ways in which men and women are different? How can these differences be put to use creatively for the benefit of both men and women?

3 In this account, as in the prologue, the practice of naming is used to exercise and delegate authority. Just as God named the day, night, sky, land, and sea, so God now watches to see what the man will name each creature, to see whether any of the names will identify the "strong ally" who's needed. When the ally isn't identified, God forms a new kind of creature, directly from the man.

When the man meets her, he not only gives her a name, he also recognizes himself by a new name, in relationship to her. To this point he's been called *'adam* in Hebrew ("human being"). But now he describes himself as *'ish* ("man" or "husband"). Throughout Genesis we'll see many other examples of naming and renaming as people are given new responsibilities and enter into new kinds of relationships with people and with God.

⮑ What does your own name mean? How was it chosen? What hopes, dreams, and aspirations does it express? Are you aware of a spiritual significance behind the meaning of your name?

4 Genesis doesn't explain how evil could exist in a good world created by an all-powerful God. But the book demonstrates very clearly how evil spreads. The serpent is the first creature to question and contradict God's authoritative word. The serpent portrays God's motives as deceptive and selfish, and he gets the woman and man to join him in questioning God. This leads them to conclude they can decide for themselves whether to keep God's command. They're unable to appreciate the damage they'll do to the beautifully ordered world God has established.

⮕ Re-create the conversation that likely took place between Adam and Eve as they decided to eat the fruit. You can do this individually or in pairs and then share your compositions with the others, or you can work together as a whole group to write this dialogue.

WICKEDNESS SPREADS
THROUGHOUT THE WORLD

**Book of Genesis > Account of the Heavens and the Earth
> Story of Cain
Book of Genesis > Account of Adam's Family Line**

INTRODUCTION

Genesis now documents how violence and wickedness spread rapidly throughout the world once people choose to disobey God. Humans disregard God's authority and pursue their own self-interest, destroying those who get in their way. Within only a few generations, God is saying he wishes he'd never made people in the first place.

READING

Read the next two episodes of the "account of the heavens and the earth" out loud like a play. Have people take these parts:

Cain and Abel. (This story begins, "Adam made love to his wife Eve . . .")

Narrator

Eve

the Lord

Cain

Cain and Lamech. (It begins, "Cain made love to his wife . . ." It ends, "At that time people began to call on the name of the LORD.")

Narrator

Lamech

Then read the "account of Adam's family line":

- Have one person read the title and introduction. ("This is the written account of Adam's family line . . .")
- Then have group members take turns reading the paragraphs that describe various figures' lives. (Each paragraph begins, "When X had lived Y years . . .")
- Finally, have someone read the rest of the "account of Adam's family line," the description of how human beings spread wickedness over the whole world. (It begins, "When human beings began to increase in number on the earth . . ." It ends, "But Noah found favor in the eyes of the LORD.")

DISCUSSION

1 Because he killed his brother, Cain is driven away from the ground, from the human community, and from the presence of God. He thus experiences more intensive alienation from creation, other people, and God. Cain cries out, "My punishment is more than I can bear!"

To protect him from being punished any further, God announces a sevenfold vengeance against any person who kills him. This threat of disproportionate violence is meant as a restraint. But humans soon use disproportionate violence to dominate and oppress other people. When someone wounds Lamech, he strikes back and kills him. He then threatens seventy-seven-fold violence against anyone who retaliates.

People start giving their daughters in marriage to some kind of mighty beings (exactly what they are is hard to identify) to produce "heroes" who make a name for themselves by their exploits. As the level of violence rises exponentially, it's not long before "every inclination of the thoughts of the human heart was only evil all the time" and the earth is filled with violence.

➲ Is there an appropriate proportion of violence that can be used by individuals and the state to protect people from harm, to restrain disorder, and to punish violent crimes? Or will any use of violence inevitably spiral out of control? Explain your thinking.

2 Paradoxically, even as human society disintegrates into violence, the arts flourish and technology develops. Cain's descendants make metal tools, create musical instruments, and invent tents so people can lead growing herds to new grazing areas. Humans continue to demonstrate the creativity that is one mark of the "image of God."

But how are people using the arts and technology they create? Was Lamech able to kill a younger, stronger man because his own son had made metal weapons? Was Lamech's defiant song supported by the music of stringed instruments and pipes? Was the purpose of nomadic herding to create bigger and bigger flocks, with the idea that "the person with the most cattle wins"?

➲ Which of these statements do you most agree with? Why?
    a. Technology is basically neutral. Any technology is potentially a force for good. What matters is how you use it.
    b. It's possible to have too much technology for your own good. To keep your life healthy and humane, you've got to say no to some technologies.

3 People in Western cultures typically find the genealogies (lists of names) in the Bible difficult reading. (The long lifespans reported here make this genealogy of Adam's descendants even more difficult to relate to. Various explanations have been offered for these lifespans, but this is one more aspect of Genesis that we won't seek to account for definitively.)

People in other cultures, however, often take great interest in the biblical genealogies. For them, a person's ancestry determines their place in the community. In some cultures, even young children memorize their own genealogies going back ten generations or more.

Western readers may appreciate these genealogies better when they recognize that they're not mere lists, they're an art form. Particular ancestors are selected for mention, and their names are arranged in significant ways. Here

Adam's descendants through Cain are traced to seven generations (a number of completeness that also mirrors the threats of violence). The last person on that list has three sons. Adam's descendants through Seth are traced to ten generations (another number of completeness). The last person on that list has three sons. The two genealogies are being paired to show that even though humanity in general is disintegrating into violence, there's a faithful line of people that God will be able to work with to bring redemption into the world.

➲ Would you want to live to be 800 or 900 years old if you could? Why or why not?

➲ How far back can you trace your own family line? Who are some of your distinguished relatives? Were any of your ancestors godly people whose influence has continued down through the generations?

SESSION 5

THE FLOOD

**Book of Genesis > Account of Noah >
Before and During the Flood**

This is a long session. The next is shorter. So if you don't finish this session in one meeting, you may decide to finish it in your next meeting along with session 6.

INTRODUCTION

The first part of the "account of Noah" describes a great flood that God used to destroy life on earth when it became hopelessly corrupt and violent. Noah's *legacy* is not the flood itself, but the survival of representatives of humanity and other created life, who give the world a new start.

The story of the flood is told in a form that Hebrew writers considered refined and elegant. This narrative shape, known as a *chiasm*, is built out of pairs of episodes. The first and last episodes are paired, as are the ones that lie just inside them, and so forth. Often the most important events or ideas are placed right in the middle. Here's how the flood story is structured:

A: Noah's actions in building the ark
  B: God addresses Noah: "Go into the ark"
    C: Noah and the animals enter the ark
      D: The flood waters rise
      God remembers Noah
      D: The flood waters fall
    C: Noah and the birds verify that the flood has ended
  B: God addresses Noah: "Come out of the ark"
A: Noah's actions in offering sacrifice

27

The story therefore centers on God's faithfulness in remembering his promises to Noah and preserving life in the midst of worldwide destruction.

READING

Have four people read the story of the flood. Assign one letter from A to D to each speaker and have them read the episodes identified by that letter in the diagram above. The episodes begin with these phrases:

A. "This is the account of Noah and his family."

B. "The LORD then said to Noah, 'Go into the ark.'"

C. "Noah was six hundred years old when the floodwaters came."

D. "For forty days the flood kept coming on the earth."

D. "But God remembered Noah . . ."

C. "After forty days Noah opened a window he had made in the ark."

B. "By the first day of the first month . . ."

A. "Then Noah built an altar to the LORD." (End with "multiply on the earth and increase upon it.")

DISCUSSION

1 As we read the biblical flood story, we may wonder, "How could this have happened, physically?" God must have used some extraordinary means to cause a flood of this magnitude, since ordinary rainfall, even a downpour of forty days, wouldn't be sufficient to cover all the mountains on earth.

We're not likely to learn the exact mechanism from the biblical flood story itself. As we've already noted, Genesis is written from an observational perspective that doesn't line up with our modern cosmology. Much of the universe is described here by analogy to things in human experience, so that there are "floodgates" in the sky and "springs" in the "great deep."

It may be helpful for group members to have the chance to share their current understanding of how the flood story relates to the natural world as we know it. Whatever physical explanation we arrive at, we can be confident that this account is reflecting a genuine experience of the community that trusted in God in ancient times, and that learning about this experience can help us follow God more closely today.

➲ What is the "take-home message" of the flood story for contemporary believers?

2 Another question that will probably strike us as we read the flood story is, "How could God have wiped out practically all life on earth? How could a loving God have thought he could further his purposes by annihilating practically all of humanity?"

The flood account depicts God carefully examining life on earth before taking any action. He determines it's become so corrupt it's beyond remedy. The only hope for the created world is to completely eliminate the mass of people that's irreversibly committed to wickedness and violence, and to start over with the few people who have remained faithful to God.

If we can't imagine a society or culture that's so wicked it's beyond redemption, this may be because we live at a time when we're the beneficiaries of many centuries of God's redemptive influence in the world. But at this early point in history, humanity has been allowed to develop on its own, and the choices people have made are threatening to corrupt the entire creation.

➲ How do we know when something is beyond redemption and we just need to start over? Does a time ever come when we need to stop trying to help another person?

3 Once we've heard the end of this story, we may wonder why God couldn't figure out in the first place how to keep from sending floods on the earth. (For that matter, why did God make humans in the first place, if he was only going to regret it later?) There are places in Genesis where God seems to learn things through experience. What's going on?

The Bible records the "progressive revelation" of God to humanity over many centuries. People's understanding of God grew and deepened over a long period of time. Because the accounts in the early part of Genesis were recorded early in the course of this "progressive revelation," they often portray God like a human being. In this study guide we'll consider these descriptions a reflection, even in these divinely inspired writings, of a youthful stage in humanity's understanding of who God is. We will accept this portrayal for what it is and seek to appreciate it on its own terms.

Thus, in the flood story, we'll accept that God appears to learn something. Humanity, when first created, is given the freedom to develop on its own. But people turn out to be so inclined to evil that they hopelessly corrupt the entire earth. God determines he must clean up this corruption, so he sends the flood. But afterwards, he realizes there's no point repeating the experience. Instead, God introduces measures to restrain the spread of violence and wickedness. On this basis, he's able to promise never to send another flood.

⮑ How much of this portrayal of God is still useful today? What do you think of the idea that God "learns as he goes along"? Does it diminish God for us to think that his plans are flexible and at least partly dependent on what his creatures do?

GOD'S COVENANT WITH NOAH

Book of Genesis > Account of Noah > After the Flood

INTRODUCTION

After describing the great flood, the "account of Noah" explains how God entered into a "covenant" with all of creation. A covenant is a relationship governed by solemn vows. Noah and his family serve as creation's representatives in the covenant ceremony.

The "account of Noah" then concludes by describing an embarrassing episode in Noah's life that had consequences for many future generations.

READING

Have one member of your group read aloud the description of the covenant God made with Noah and the rest of creation. (It begins, "Then God said to Noah and to his sons with him: 'I now establish my covenant . . .'")

Have another member read the story about Noah's drunkenness and its consequences. (It begins, "The sons of Noah who came out of the ark were Shem, Ham and Japheth." It ends, "Noah lived a total of 950 years, and then he died.")

DISCUSSION

1 *Covenant* is one of the most important concepts in the book of Genesis. It's used to structure the unfolding relationship between God and humanity. In our own societies we're probably more used to *contracts*, agreements between parties enforceable by law. But in biblical times, people made covenants instead, which were agreements enforceable by God. (The informal equivalent today is to guarantee a promise by saying, "I swear to God and hope to die!")

There were two types of covenants. A one-way or unconditional covenant was a solemn promise by one person to do something for another person, no questions asked. In a two-way or conditional covenant, the parties promised to do something for one another, so long as each party kept its end of the deal.

Here God makes a one-way covenant with all of creation. He says, "I establish my covenant with you: Never again will all life be destroyed by the waters of a flood." God thus guarantees the promises he made at the end of the flood story.

➲ What's the best promise you remember someone making to you and keeping?

2 Covenants are typically confirmed with signs or tokens that symbolize their obligations. God says that the "rainbow in the clouds" will serve as a sign of this covenant. The term translated "rainbow" here is exactly the same word used in Hebrew for "bow" as a weapon ("bow and arrow"). So this sign means that God is "hanging up his weapons" of cloud and rain and won't ever use them to destroy the whole earth again.

➲ What contemporary examples can you give, from your own experience or from films or television programs you've seen or from books you've read, of signs or tokens that guarantee promises?

3 In the Garden of Eden, there was perfect mutuality and transparency between the first human pair, so that they were "naked and felt no shame." But as soon as their relationships were broken by disobedience to God, they tried to hide their nakedness. This is because, in a fallen world, nakedness represents vulnerability to other beings who must be considered potentially hostile and exploitive until proven otherwise.

Ham's actions against his father Noah confirm this picture. Ham tries to embarrass and discredit his father to advance himself at Noah's expense. In response, Noah speaks curses and blessings designed to restrain the part of his own family line that is showing a revived tendency towards wickedness.

➲ What different things does nakedness or near-nakedness signify in our culture? In what contexts is a person's nakedness used to exploit or demean them, and in what contexts is it used to affirm them?

HUMANITY IS DIVIDED INTO NATIONS

Book of Genesis > Account of Shem, Ham, and Japheth
Book of Genesis > Account of Shem

INTRODUCTION

To this point in the book of Genesis, God has been dealing with humanity as a whole. But now God makes a transition and begins dealing with one representative part of humanity, in order to reach out to all nations through it. This transition takes place over the course of the next two "accounts" in Genesis.

The "account of Shem, Ham and Japheth" describes how various nations "spread out over the earth after the flood." It then backs up to explain why they were scattered, instead of remaining one unified human community.

The "account of Shem" narrows down the focus and traces the descendants of Noah's son Shem down to the representative figure God will begin dealing with, Abram (Abraham).

READING

As we've seen, the genealogies in the Bible aren't just lists, they're an art form. Names are selected and arranged to create patterns that symbolically communicate a message. Recurring phrases create an overall structure and provide pacing along the way. As you read through the genealogy of Noah's sons, follow the diagram on page 36.

Note that this genealogy has a matching opening and closing. Its three sections are introduced and concluded by standard formulas.

Have one person read the opening and closing sentences of this genealogy. Have three other people read the sections that describe the descendants of Japheth, Ham, and Shem:

⭐ *Opening sentence.* ("This is the account of Shem, Ham and Japheth, Noah's sons, who themselves had sons after the flood.")

⭐ *Japheth.* ("The sons of Japheth . . . by their clans within their nations, each with its own language.")

⭐ *Ham.* (The sons of Ham . . . the sons of Ham by their clans and languages, in their territories and nations.")

⭐ *Shem.* ("Sons were also born to Shem . . . the sons of Shem by their clans and languages, in their territories and nations.")

⭐ *Closing sentences.* ("These are the clans of Noah's sons . . .")

Then have another person read the story of the Tower of Babel. (It begins, "Now the whole world had one language and a common speech.")

Finally, take turns reading the paragraphs in the "account of Shem's family line." (These follow the same formula as the earlier genealogy of Adam's descendants: "When X had lived Y years . . ." End with, "he became the father of Abram, Nahor and Haran.")

GENEALOGY OF NOAH'S SONS

This is the account of Shem, Ham and Japheth, **Noah's sons**, who themselves had sons **after the flood**.

The sons of Japheth . . .

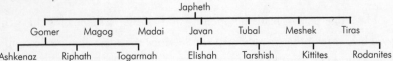

. . . spread out into their **territories** by their **clans** within their **nations**, each with its own **language**.

The sons of Ham . . .

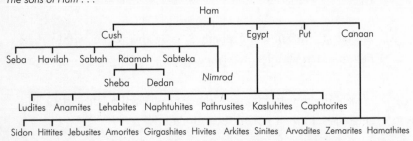

These are the sons of Ham by their **clans** and **languages**, in their **territories** and **nations**.

The sons of Shem . . .

These are the sons of Shem by their **clans** and **languages**, in their **territories** and **nations**.

These are the clans of **Noah's** sons, according to their lines of descent, within their nations. From these the nations spread out over the earth **after the flood**.

Diagrams based on Gordon Wenham, Genesis 1-15, *Word Biblical Commentary 1* (Dallas: Word Books, 1987), pp. 216, 220, 229.

DISCUSSION

1 Even after the flood judgment, humanity remains defiant against God. People develop the technology to make bricks—uniformly shaped building blocks that will permit them to raise, on the flat plain they find, a vastly higher tower than they could make with wood or stone. Their goal is to "reach to the heavens" and establish themselves where God lives. They want to "make a name" for themselves and be renowned throughout the earth.

God "comes down" to see what they're doing (this is one more portrayal in Genesis of God in human terms). He realizes that humanity is united in its determination to seize as many divine prerogatives for itself as it can. So God confuses their languages. Unable to understand one another, the people abandon their common project and scatter over the whole earth.

➲ What would today's world be like if all of humanity was still united? How would the world be organized? What projects do you think humanity would pursue?

➲ What's lost, and what's gained, because the people of the world speak many different languages?

➲ How does mass-production affect the quality of human work? Compare the experience of a worker at Babel, who spent all day making brick after brick, with the experience of tending the Garden of Eden. Is it possible to have the benefits of mass production and still maintain a high quality of life in the workplace?

2 The ancient world believed that humanity was made up of seventy different nations. The "account of Shem, Ham and Japheth" describes where these nations came from. Seventy ancestors of nations are listed. (This total doesn't include Nimrod, who's not the *ancestor* of a nation, but a distinguished descendant of Ham who founded great cities including Nineveh and Babylon.)

We are about to be introduced to the family that God will enter into a special covenant with. By the end of Genesis, this family will have seventy people in it. This description of the nations thus prepares us to recognize Abraham's family as a microcosm of humanity, and to see worldwide significance in the way God builds a relationship with them.

➲ Which of these statements best describes how you feel about the biblical genealogies?

a. Now that I've learned more about how they work, I find them fascinating.

b. I appreciate them a little bit better.

c. They're dry as dust and I still don't understand why God put them in the Bible.

ABRAHAM

ABRAM ANSWERS GOD'S CALL AND TRAVELS TO THE LAND OF CANAAN

**Book of Genesis > Account of Terah >
Abraham Story, Episodes 1 and 2**

INTRODUCTION

The "account of Terah" is actually the story of his son Abram (later called Abraham), whose life and faith were the great legacy that Terah left to the world. God will establish a relationship with Abram and use it to invite all people back into relationship with himself. God calls Abram to leave his family and homeland so he can begin a new nation through him. Abram obeys this call and travels to the new land that God promises to give him.

Most of the story of Abraham's life is told in the same literary form as the flood story, that is, in a *chiasm* built out of pairs of parallel episodes. While the birth of Ishmael, as the central episode, would ordinarily have the highest importance, in this case the event related in the final episode, the birth of Isaac, exceeds it in significance.

This chiasm is so long that we'll consider it over the course of the next six studies. We'll begin in this study with the first two episodes.

A: God promises to bless Abram; he travels to the land of Canaan

  B: Abram moves temporarily to Egypt; Sarah taken by Pharaoh

    C: Lot is rescued after Sodom is raided

      D: God makes a covenant with Abram

        E: Ishmael is born

      D: God confirms his covenant with Abraham

    C: Lot is rescued when Sodom is destroyed

  B: Abraham moves temporarily to Gerar; Sarah taken by Abimelek

A: Isaac is born, fulfilling God's first promises to Abraham

READING

The first two episodes in the story of Abram trace the stages of the journey he made from his homeland in Ur through the land of Canaan, down into Egypt, and then back into Canaan to settle there. Have six different people read the descriptions of these stages. As you read, you can follow Abram's journey on the map on page 43.

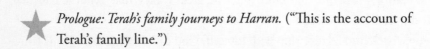

Prologue: Terah's family journeys to Harran. ("This is the account of Terah's family line.")

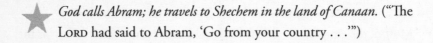

God calls Abram; he travels to Shechem in the land of Canaan. ("The LORD had said to Abram, 'Go from your country . . .'")

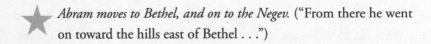

Abram moves to Bethel, and on to the Negev. ("From there he went on toward the hills east of Bethel . . .")

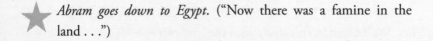

Abram goes down to Egypt. ("Now there was a famine in the land . . .")

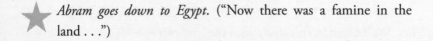

Abram leaves Egypt and returns to Bethel. ("So Abram went up from Egypt to the Negev . . .")

ABRAM'S JOURNEY TO CANAAN

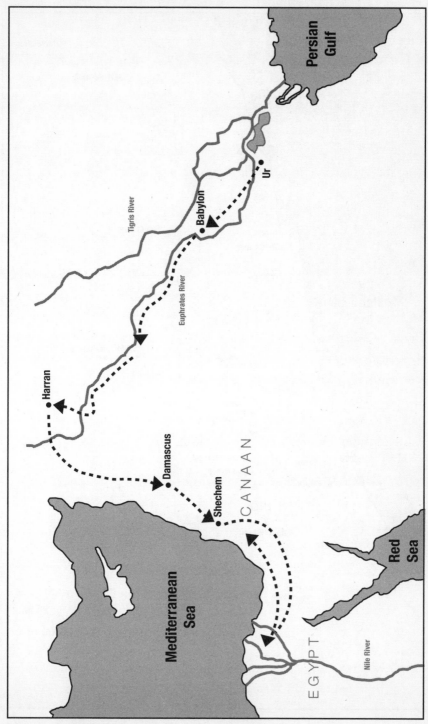

Persian Gulf

Tigris River

Babylon

Euphrates River

Ur

Harran

Damascus

Shechem

CANAAN

Mediterranean Sea

Red Sea

EGYPT

Nile River

ABRAM'S JOURNEY THROUGH CANAAN

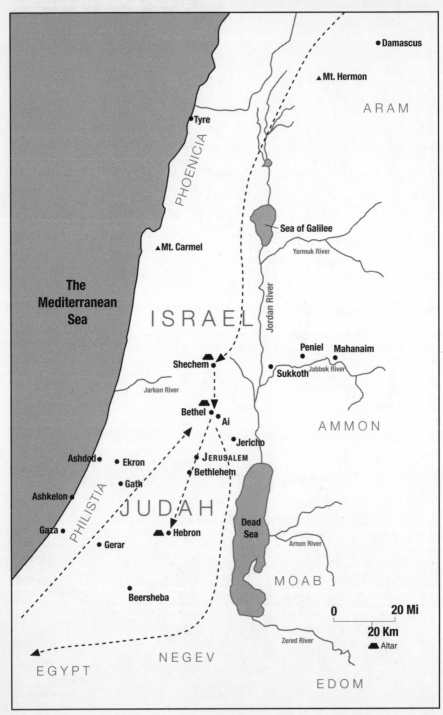

Abram moves to Hebron. ("So Abram went to live near the great trees of Mamre . . . There he built an altar to the LORD.")

DISCUSSION

1 God explains to Abram that he wants to reach out through him to the whole world: "all peoples on earth will be blessed through you." Instead of dealing with the entire human race at once, God will be engaging a representative group and inviting the rest of the world to join in his relationship with them.

⊃ Even though God is reaching out to the entire world here, he's still creating a single way for people to enter into a relationship with him. This is different from the idea that "all paths lead to God." What do you think about this?

a. There's only one way to come to God, and it's by becoming part of the story told in the Bible.
b. People might be taking the one path without knowing it.
c. All of the world's religions are potentially ways that people can truly meet God.
d. I'm not exactly sure what I think.

2 Abram walks all through the land as a sign that it will one day belong to his offspring. As the map on page 44 shows, he comes into the land of Canaan from the north, travels all the way through it, and builds altars to God at a couple of central locations and at the southern end. By worshipping God in these locations, Abram is proclaiming that the whole land is under God's authority and will belong to the people God had chosen to give it to. Abram's journey to and through Canaan was thus an expression of his faith and confidence that God would fulfill his promises.

⊃ What promises or purposes are you waiting for God to fulfill in your life? If you wanted to express your confidence in God's purposes for your life through pilgrimage and worship, how could you do this?

3 Even though Abram demonstrates great faith in most of these episodes, he fears for his life when he's in Egypt. In this culture, foreigners had no rights and no protection, and they were liable to be exploited and victimized. Abram gets Sarah to say that she's his sister, not his wife, so that no one will kill him to take her away. As a result, he loses her for a time into Pharaoh's harem. It's disturbing to see God's chosen representative of humanity practice such cowardice and deception.

➲ What's going on in this episode? (Choose one of the answers below, or provide your own.)

a. The only kind of people God has to work with are imperfect ones, and they're going to make big mistakes from time to time. We have to cut Abram some slack. In the overall scheme of things, he's still a faithful man.

b. Abram didn't trust God or tell the truth, and Sarai was treated like a commodity, but they got really rich through all of this, so maybe it worked out all right in the end.

c. This episode is a symbolic foreshadowing of the exodus, when the Egyptians take Abram's descendants captive and God delivers them through plagues. It's not meant to be taken too literally.

d. I don't get it. Abram does wrong, but he gets rich. Pharaoh was innocent, but he got struck with a plague. It's not fair. How can God do this?

NOTE

Another controversial question arising from Genesis is whether God's promises to Abram here mean that the modern nation of Israel has an exclusive claim on the land of Palestine. This is one more matter of interpretation the group should encourage each member to have a thoughtful opinion about, but not debate.

GOD GIVES ABRAM VICTORY IN BATTLE AND PROMISES HIM A SON

Book of Genesis > Account of Terah > Abraham Story, Episodes 3 and 4

INTRODUCTION

In this study we'll look at the next two episodes in the "account of Terah." In the outline in session 8, they correspond to:

> C. Lot is rescued after Sodom is raided
> > D. God makes a covenant with Abram

In these episodes, God fulfills and extends his promises to Abram. Abram begins to become a blessing to others, just as God said he would.

READING

Read aloud the story of Abraham rescuing Lot when he was captured by Kedorlaomer and his allies. Have the members of your group take turns reading one paragraph each. (The story begins, "At the time when Amraphel was king of Shinar . . ." and continues through Abram's dealings with Melchizedek and with the king of Sodom.)

As you read, you can follow the action on the map on page 48.

ABRAM RESCUES LOT FROM THE FOUR MESOPOTAMIAN KINGS

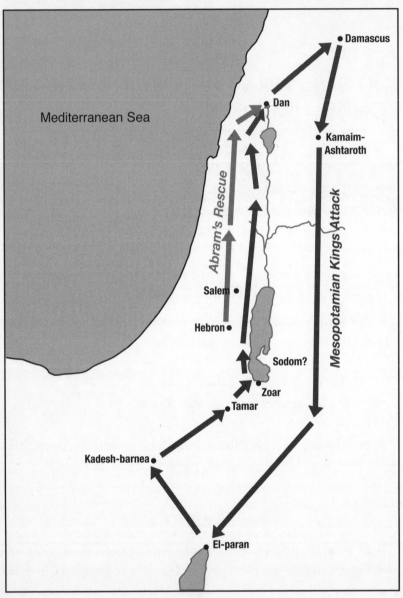

Map based on Ralph F. Wilson, "Abraham Rescues His Nephew Lot," http://www.jesuswalk.com/abraham/3_rescue.htm

Then read the story that follows about God's renewed promises to Abram. Read it out loud like a play. (You can leave out brief narrative cues like "He also said to him," and "But Abram said.") The parts are:

Narrator

the LORD

Abram

(The narrator begins, "After this, the word of the LORD came to Abram . . ." The scene ends with the LORD saying, ". . . Canaanites, Girgashites and Jebusites.")

DISCUSSION

1 It's remarkable that Abram could defeat the combined armies of four kingdoms with a force of just 318 household servants. He did have some help from his allies Aner, Eshkol, and Mamre. His forces also had the element of surprise in a night attack. Armies returning from a victorious campaign sometimes let down their guard. Nevertheless, Abram's victory is still stunning.

Melchizedek gives the true explanation: "God Most High . . . delivered your enemies into your hand." God had promised to help anyone who was on Abram's side, and oppose anyone who was against him. God keeps this promise here and rescues Lot and his family for Abram's sake.

Melchizedek, recognizing what God has done, serves a ceremonial meal and blesses Abram in God's name. Abram responds by worshipping God. He gives God a tenth of the recaptured goods, in care of this priest.

The king of Sodom also has the chance to recognize the way God is at work here, but he's thinking only about how much of the plunder he can get. He demands his subjects back and offers to let Abram keep spoils that are already rightfully his. But Abram gives back everything the invaders carried off.

⮕ Why do you think Abram didn't want to keep anything that belonged to the king of Sodom?

➲ Has a friend or relative been able to recognize God's work in your life and celebrate it with you, as Melchizedek does with Abram here? If so, describe how they did this.

2 In earlier parts of Genesis we've encountered two divine names: *'Elohim*, the general word for "God," and *Yahweh* ("I AM"), a name that God would later use in making a covenant with Abram's descendants. Most English translations render *Yahweh* as "the LORD" in small caps. (Even though God wasn't known by the name *Yahweh* in Abram's time, the Genesis narrator used it to show later generations that their ancestors knew and served the same God they did.)

Now a third name is introduced. Melchizedek speaks of *'El 'Elyon*, "God Most High." This refers to the supreme God, the "creator of heaven and earth." Melchizedek knew something about God by the way creation demonstrated his existence and power. But Melchizedek now understands God better and more personally through his faithfulness to his covenant relationship with Abram.

➲ What do you think of this statement: "God will honor the sincere devotion of those who worship him with the light they have. God will bring them into the community of people that he's working through to reach out to the whole world"?

3 When God speaks to Abram after this battle, he first confirms that he was the one who won the victory for him. (God says he's Abram's "shield." The term comes from the same root as Melchizedek's word "delivered.")

God then promises that even though Abram gave away all the spoils, he will still have a "very great reward." Abram responds that he has no children of his own to pass this reward on to. God counters that he will give Abram a son to be his heir. When Abram believes this unlikely promise, this is "credited to him as righteousness." Abram's implicit faith and trust in God show he's in an authentic relationship with God.

➲ Genesis doesn't record what Abram actually said in response to God's promise to give him as many descendants as the stars in the sky. Have each person in your group reconstruct the missing line(s) of dialogue by writing out what Abram may have said. Anyone who wants to can share what they wrote with the rest of the group.

4 To confirm his promise to Abram, God enters into a covenant with him. While the word *covenant* isn't used explicitly, the ceremony that's performed here is the one that was used in the ancient world to ratify a covenant. The participants would walk between the severed pieces of sacrificial animals to say, "May I be torn apart like this if I fail to keep this covenant!"

Since God is making a one-way, unconditional covenant with Abram here, God alone walks between the pieces, appearing in the form of a firepot and blazing torch.

⊃ What do you think of a God who agrees to become "buzzard bait" if he doesn't keep his word?

ISHMAEL IS BORN; GOD GIVES A COVENANT SIGN AND NEW NAMES

Book of Genesis > Account of Terah > Abraham Story, Episodes 5 and 6

INTRODUCTION

The next two episodes in the "account of Terah" pursue the question of who will be Abram's heir. Recall the outline in session 8:

E. Ishmael is born
D. God confirms his covenant with Abraham

Sarai plots to have an adoptive child by giving her servant Hagar to Abram as a secondary wife, as was permitted in this culture. This plan will have many destructive consequences for all of them. Some years later, God renews and deepens his covenant with Abram, promising to give him a son through Sarai and to extend the covenant to that son and to all of his descendants.

READING

Read the story of Hagar out loud like a play. (It begins, "Now Sarai, Abram's wife, had borne him no children." It ends, "Abram was eighty-six years old when Hagar bore him Ishmael.") The parts are:

Narrator
Sarai
Abram
angel of the LORD
Hagar

Then have someone read the story of God's renewed covenant with Abram. (It begins, "When Abram was ninety-nine years old . . ." and ends, "And every male in Abraham's household, including those born in his household or bought from a foreigner, was circumcised with him.")

DISCUSSION

1 Sarai decides to use means of her own to get the son God has promised. In this culture, a female slave could become a secondary wife, and the first wife could claim her children. Sarai suggests doing this with Hagar, and Abram agrees.

But when Hagar conceives a child, Sarai becomes bitter and jealous. Abram doesn't defend Hagar, even though she's legally his wife. Instead, he abandons her to Sarai's mistreatment. Doubly victimized, Hagar flees into the desert, but ultimately she has to return to a very difficult situation. Nevertheless, she goes back with the knowledge that God sees and understands her circumstances, and with God's promise to make her son formidable and free. The name God gives her son, Ishmael, means "God hears." And Hagar gives God a new name: *'El Ro'eh*, "the God who sees."

⮑ Abraham and Sarah victimize and abuse Hagar because of their lack of faith. Nevertheless, Hagar's own relationship with God deepens and strengthens through this difficult experience. When we're let down or abused by people who supposedly represent God, how can we keep this from damaging our own faith? How does Hagar provide a positive example for us?

⮑ If you could give God a name to express how you've come to know him better through difficult times, what would that name be?

53

2 Many years later, God speaks to Abram to renew and extend his covenant with him. God introduces himself by a new name, *El Shaddai* ("God Almighty"). This name expresses his strength and power to fulfill his promises.

God also gives Abram and Sarai new names. Abram means "exalted father." God changes this to Abraham, "father of a multitude," to express his purpose to make Abraham "very fruitful," the "father of many nations." And God changes the name Sarai to Sarah, a more recognizable form of the word meaning "princess," since "kings of peoples will come from her." Through these new names, God expresses and guarantees the purposes he'll fulfill in their lives. The names are, in effect, miniature covenant vows.

⟩ Has your name ever changed? If so, under what circumstances? What new relationship, responsibility, or role was expressed in your name change? Have your friends or family given you a new name or nickname that expresses the possibilities God has built into your life? Do you have an e-mail address, blog or Twitter name, etc., that's a self-chosen "new name" that expresses some distinctive that God has built into your life?

3 In addition to guaranteeing his covenant with new names, God also guarantees it with a sign, just as he gave the sign of the rainbow for his covenant with Noah.

God uses the sign of circumcision to guarantee his covenant with Abraham, to symbolize how this covenant wasn't just with Abraham, but also with his son and with all of their descendants, perpetually. The sign would be replicated in the bodies of all future generations: "My covenant *in your flesh* is to be an *everlasting* covenant" (italics added).

⟩ Families that practiced circumcision showed that they belonged to the community that was created by God's covenant with Abraham. A new kind of community has since been created by God's covenant with Jesus, and it has a new sign of its own. Baptism is the sign of belonging to the community of Jesus' followers. How does baptism signify God's obligations to us under the "new covenant," and our obligations to him? There's a suggested answer that you can interact with in the note at the end of this session.

(The rest of the Bible tells the story of how the covenant with Abraham was expanded and extended through covenants with Moses and David, and how a "new covenant" with Jesus ultimately transcended and transformed it. If you're new to the Bible, you won't have all of this background yet. But keep reading—you'll be excited by what you discover.)

NOTE

Question 3: Baptism symbolizes God's covenant obligations to us by illustrating his promise to raise us from the dead, both physically (when we die) and spiritually (as we experience new life in Christ). Baptism symbolizes our covenant obligations to God by illustrating the way followers of Jesus are supposed to die to sin and rise to a new life of faith and obedience.

ABRAHAM'S THREE VISITORS

**Book of Genesis > Account of Terah >
Abraham Story, Episode 7**

INTRODUCTION

In the next two sessions, we'll look at the next episode in the chiasm that tells the story of most of Abraham's life:

C: Lot is rescued when Sodom is destroyed

As this episode begins, Abraham is still living in Hebron. One day three strangers arrive at his tent. These mysterious figures are a manifestation or embodiment of God himself. (God appears to people in forms like this several times in Genesis. The "angel of the LORD" who spoke with Hagar was a similar figure.) Abraham shows his visitors generous hospitality and discovers they've come to confirm God's promise to give him and Sarah a son. There's also an urgent matter of justice that God wants to talk to Abraham about.

READING

Read the story of Abraham's three visitors out loud like a play. (It begins, "The LORD appeared to Abraham near the great trees of Mamre . . ." It ends,

"When the LORD had finished speaking with Abraham, he left, and Abraham returned home.") The parts are:

> Narrator
> Abraham
> the visitors (= the LORD)
> Sarah

DISCUSSION

1 Abraham doesn't know who these three travelers are, but he offers them the warm hospitality that was an ideal in his culture. He presents himself as their "servant," and modestly understates what he wants to offer them. He promises them "something to eat" (literally "a little bread"), but this turns out to be an elaborate banquet. Abraham's welcome creates a setting where the visitors can repeat the promise God had made to him: About this time the next year, he and Sarah will have a son.

⮥ Can you think of a time when you received lavish and gracious hospitality like this, even as a "stranger"? When?

⮥ This is one of many examples in the Bible where hospitality is extended and enjoyed before important business is transacted. What values does this approach express? In what contexts does your own culture also reflect these values? Is there ever a time to "dispense with the formalities and get right down to business"?

2 When Sarah, listening from the tent, hears the promise that she'll have a son, she laughs. It's just too impossible to believe. In the previous episode, Abraham himself laughed when God told him the same thing. And so God said the boy should be named Isaac, which means "he laughs." The idea behind the name is probably, "God can do things that seem so impossible people laugh when they hear about them." The same idea is put another way here: "Is anything too hard for the LORD?"

⮑ What's the most "impossible" thing you've seen God do for you, or for someone you know? Is there a situation in your life that you can trust God to do more about than you've previously imagined, if nothing is "too hard for the LORD"?

⮑ Why do you think Sarah was afraid and denied that she laughed?

3 As Abraham sees his visitors off, God raises one more important matter. He's heard an "outcry" against the sins and crimes of Sodom and Gomorrah, and he's come down to see whether this report is true. The implication is that God will destroy these cities if they're as wicked as he's heard. But God talks this plan over first with Abraham, since he's humanity's representative in the relationship that God is rebuilding with them.

This gives Abraham the opportunity to advocate for the people living in these cities, including his nephew Lot and his family. Through an intricate negotiation, showing both deference and tenacity, Abraham gets God to agree not to destroy the cities if even ten righteous people are living there.

⮑ Does God want to consult with people who know him as he determines the right balance of justice and mercy in dealing with humanity? Or is God just going to do what he's going to do, without asking what we think?

⮑ Will God still spare a community or organization if a certain number of "righteous" people are in it? What makes someone "righteous" in this way?

SODOM AND GOMORRAH

**Book of Genesis > Account of Terah >
Abraham Story, Episode 7 continued**

INTRODUCTION

The two "men" who accompanied the LORD on this investigative mission turn out to be angels. They travel to Sodom, and find it every bit as evil and violent as they've heard. Threatened with gang-rape by a mob of every man who lives there (there aren't even ten righteous ones), the angels pull Lot and his family away, and God destroys Sodom and the surrounding cities by fire. But Lot and his family then show how deeply they've been influenced by the place where they've been living.

Note: The story of Sodom and Gomorrah has often been understood as a depiction of God's judgment against the practice of homosexuality. (The term *sodomy* is derived from this story.) This practice should be understood in light of the Bible's overall teaching about human sexuality. However, it isn't actually being considered in this story. The gang-rape that the men of Sodom attempt is like the ones that are sometimes attempted in prisons today. These don't reflect a same-sex attraction. Instead, they're acts of violence that a group uses to brutalize and degrade others, to assert their power over them. So the practice of homosexuality will not be raised as a point of discussion in connection with this story. However, if your group thinks it would be helpful, people can take turns respectfully stating, if they wish, their own beliefs about the issue.

READING

Read the story of Sodom and Gomorrah like a play. (It begins, "The two angels arrived at Sodom in the evening . . ." It continues through the destruction of Sodom, Lot's flight, and the incident between Lot and his daughters. It ends, "he is the father of the Ammonites of today.") The parts are:

> Narrator
> Lot
> the angels
> the men of Sodom
> Lot's older daughter

(Fair warning: these aren't the kind of reading parts they used to give out for the Sunday School Christmas pageant.)

DISCUSSION

1 Just as the flood story gave special prominence to the statement that "God remembered Noah," the concluding summary of the Sodom and Gomorrah story describes how God rescued Lot. The emphasis of the narrative is that in the midst of judgment, God shows mercy. Nevertheless, it's disturbing to read that God sent fire from heaven to burn up all the people who were living in several cities. The book of Genesis is careful to show that these extreme measures were only taken in response to a situation of outrageous and irremediable evil.

⊃ What indications are there, in this story and the one about Abraham and his visitors, that Sodom and Gomorrah couldn't be reformed, and that God carefully determined this before destroying them? (Some suggested answers are offered in the note below.)

⮑ If there is such a thing as a "point of no return," when a person or group can't be brought back to God anymore, how do we keep from ever getting near that point? What are the danger signs that it's approaching?

2 Another very disturbing element of this story is Lot's offer to give his virgin daughters to the mob. "Let me bring them out to you," he says, "and you can do what you like with them."

⮑ How could a father even contemplate doing such a thing to his own daughters? Choose the answer(s) that you think make sense, or suggest one of your own:

a. This shows what a low view of women this culture had. Women were treated as just another piece of property.

b. Lot might have understood the responsibilities of hospitality, but he certainly didn't understand that his responsibility to protect his family came first.

c. Lot didn't expect the mob to take him seriously when he made this offer. He wanted to shock them into recognizing what a wicked thing they had in mind.

d. Lot was so desperate to save his own skin he would have given his own daughters to a mob! He's weak, lazy, and cowardly in the rest of the story, too. It could only have been for Abraham's sake that God spared him at all.

e. It's absolutely incomprehensible to me how a father could do such a thing.

f. Some of the fathers I know would be capable of this.

3 Lot's family has been so influenced by life in Sodom that his daughters think incest is an appropriate way for them to have children.

⮑ What values does our culture communicate to children and youth about human sexuality? What channels does this cultural influence flow through? How can the community of Jesus' followers teach and model a healthy understanding of sexuality?

LEADER'S NOTE

Question 1: God comes down in person to see what's happening in Sodom, and his representatives experience first hand how the city oppresses helpless people.

God also grants Abraham's repeated requests not to destroy the righteous with the wicked, and promises to spare the cities if even ten righteous citizens can be found. (They can't.)

Third, God is described as the "Judge of all the earth" who "does right." By contrast, the men of Sodom reject Lot's protests, calling him a would-be "judge" they don't have to listen to. Their sense of right and wrong is entirely backwards.

Fourth, Lot's future sons-in-law laugh at what they consider the impossibility of judgment.

Finally, Lot is so affected by Sodom that he ends up pleading for a few wicked to be spared (in the city of Zoar), in contrast to the way Abraham had pleaded for the righteous to be spared.

ABRAHAM MOVES INTO THE NEGEV REGION; ISAAC IS BORN

Book of Genesis > Account of Terah > Abraham Story, Episodes 8 and 9 with aftermath

INTRODUCTION

In this study we'll look at the final two episodes in the chiasm that tells most of Abraham's life story:

> B: Abraham moves temporarily to Gerar; Sarah taken by Abimelek
>
> A: Isaac is born, fulfilling God's first promises to Abraham

We'll also begin looking at the short series of episodes that follow the chiasm. These episodes relate the final events of Abraham's life.

READING

Have four different people read four stories aloud:

 Abimelek takes Sarah into the royal harem. (It begins, "Now Abraham moved on from there into the region of the Negev . . .")

Isaac is born. (It begins, "Now the LORD was gracious to Sarah . . .")

 Hagar is sent away into the desert. (It begins, "The child grew and was weaned, and on the day Isaac was weaned . . .")

 Abraham and Abimelek make a treaty. (It begins, "At that time Abimelek and Phicol . . ." It ends, "And Abraham stayed in the land of the Philistines for a long time.")

(You can located places like Gerar and the Negev on the map accompanying session 8.)

DISCUSSION

1 How could Abraham make exactly the same mistake twice, and tell the people of Gerar that Sarah was his sister, not his wife, after all the trouble this caused in Egypt? Witnessing the destruction of Sodom and Gomorrah had to be a horrifying experience for Abraham. Externally, he's able to "move on" from it by relocating. But internally, he's still deeply affected by it, and it makes him regress to old, unhealthy strategies for survival.

⮑ How can people make a new start on the inside and get free from the influence of past traumatic experiences?

⮑ How could Abraham have kept from assuming that the people of Gerar would be just like the people of Sodom and try to victimize him as a foreigner?

2 With the birth of Isaac, the long-awaited son arrives. Sarah gives a new interpretation to his name. Instead of reflecting the shameful laughter of incredulity, it now expresses the joy of a promise fulfilled: "Everyone who hears about this will laugh with me."

⮑ Several times in Genesis a person's name is changed; here a name is given a new, positive interpretation. Have you or someone you know found new meaning in a name, word, symbol, place, or time as a result of God's work in your life? Explain.

3 For a second time, Hagar has to leave Abraham's encampment and wander into the desert. This time, she can never return. When her supplies run out, Hagar expects that she and her son will die. But once again the "angel of God" speaks with her. God fulfills the promise in the name he gave her son: Ishmael, "God hears." "God has heard the boy crying," the angel assures Hagar, and will save his life and "make him into a great nation." God shows Hagar where to find water, and she and Ishmael begin to make a new life for themselves in the desert.

⮑ Rank the characters in this story from best to worst. (In alphabetical order, they're Abraham, God/the angel of God, Hagar, Isaac, Ishmael, and Sarah.) Defend your ranking by explaining what the "worst" characters should have done differently, and what the "best" ones did right.

4 When Abimelek asks Abraham to make a treaty with him, this fulfills another promise God has made, that he and his descendants will be able to live in this land.

The treaty confirms Abraham's ownership of the well at Beersheba. These "water rights" are crucial for survival in this arid region. Just as Hagar found a well to save Ishmael's life, Abraham acquires a well for his descendants through Isaac.

With the future looking more secure than ever, Abraham worships God under a new name, *El 'Olam*, "the Eternal God." The reference isn't to God's eternal past existence, but to God's perpetual future presence with Abraham's descendants.

⮑ Look ahead several generations into the future. Picture the descendants of your own family and friends meeting the same God we can know today. How do you imagine God interacting with them? What do you imagine God doing for them?

GOD TELLS ABRAHAM TO SACRIFICE ISAAC; THE DEATH AND BURIAL OF SARAH

**Book of Genesis > Account of Terah >
Abraham Story, Later Episodes**

INTRODUCTION

Genesis now describes how Abraham demonstrated his faith and trust in God when he was asked to sacrifice his son Isaac. Abraham's willingness to obey even the most difficult instructions leads to a renewal and expansion of God's promises to bless him, and to bless the whole world through him.

Then, as the lengthy "account of Terah" approaches its conclusion, its main characters begin to leave the stage, while new characters, who will figure in later accounts, are introduced.

READING

Read, out loud like a play, the story of God testing Abraham. (It begins, "Some time later, God tested Abraham.") The parts are:

Narrator
God/the angel of the LORD
Abraham
Isaac

Then have someone read the brief genealogy that introduces Rebekah. (It begins, "Some time later Abraham was told, 'Milkah is also a mother.'")

Finally, read the story of Abraham buying a burial cave for Sarah. (It begins, "Sarah lived to be a hundred and twenty-seven years old." It ends, "So the field and the cave in it were deeded to Abraham by the Hittites as a burial site.") The parts are:

Narrator
Abraham
the Hittites
Ephron

DISCUSSION

1 It's disturbing to hear God tell Abraham to offer Isaac as a human sacrifice. But this story is actually intended to provide a powerful illustration *forbidding* human sacrifice. God didn't come up with this idea as a way of testing Abraham. Rather, he used an already-existing practice of the surrounding nations to give Abraham the opportunity to show that everything he had was completely devoted to God. But God then made it very clear he did not want any human sacrifices.

⮑ Was it fair for God to ask Abraham to sacrifice Isaac, when God really didn't want him to? Does God sometimes guide us in a certain direction not because he actually wants us to go that way, but for some other purpose?

⮑ This story has often been seen as a foreshadowing of how God provided Jesus as a substitute, to die in our place so that we could have new life by following him. Explain how this story can provide an analogy to illustrate what Jesus has done for us.

2 When God "tests" Abraham here, the idea isn't that Abraham needs to pass a certain "test" in order to be approved or accepted by God. Instead, the Hebrew word refers to an opportunity for training, exercise, or greater experience. It's like taking a car out on the open road to "let it show what it's got under the hood." God knows how devoted and obedient Abraham is, and he gives him the opportunity to display those qualities openly.

⮕ What things are you currently experiencing in your own life that you'd describe as "tests"? Can you look at them in a new way: if God isn't "testing" you to see whether you'll fail, but rather to allow you to display admirable qualities he already sees in you, what qualities do your present "tests" give you the opportunity to exhibit in new and stronger ways?

⮕ An ancient application of this story seems to have been that we can trust God to provide in unforeseen ways when we step out in obedience. This story gave rise to a popular saying, "On the mountain of the LORD it will be provided." (That is, when we get to the place where God wants us, what we need will be provided.) Have you ever had an experience where you followed God's leading first, and then received what you needed? What happened?

ABRAHAM'S SERVANT FINDS REBEKAH AS A WIFE FOR ISAAC; THE DEATH OF ABRAHAM

**Book of Genesis > Account of Terah >
Abraham Story, Final Episodes**

INTRODUCTION

As the "account of Terah" concludes, it describes how God led Abraham's senior servant to find a special kind of wife for Isaac. Following the example his master set throughout his life, Abraham's servant trusts God to lead him providentially. He finds just the right young woman: Rebekah.

Once she returns to Canaan and marries Isaac, Abraham's life work is done. Even though he's had more children by another wife, he makes Isaac his undisputed heir and, leaving Isaac to take the next steps in making this family a blessing to all nations, Abraham joins his first wife Sarah in death.

READING

Read aloud like a play the story of Abraham's servant going to find a wife for Isaac. (It begins, "Abraham was now very old, and the LORD had blessed him . . .") The parts are:

Narrator

Abraham

the servant

Rebekah

Laban

Bethuel (Laban's father)

Laban's mother

(Laban's father and mother never speak alone. Each of them speaks along with Laban. In those cases, the readers can speak together.)

Then have someone read the genealogy of Keturah's children. (It begins, "Abraham had taken another wife, whose name was Keturah.")

Finally, have someone read the description of Abraham's death and burial. (It begins, "Abraham lived a hundred and seventy-five years" and ends, "Beer Lahai Roi.")

DISCUSSION

1 Abraham's servant had to find a woman among Abraham's relatives back in Harran who would be willing to marry a clan member living at a great distance from her family home. Only with God's help could he fulfill an assignment like this. Abraham tells him God will "send his angel before you," and the servant himself prays, "LORD . . . make me successful today." (Literally, "make things happen ahead of me"!) Then, trusting God to be at work, he asks for a particular sign. If a young woman is so hospitable, hard-working, and generous that she offers to water all of the camels, may this be the woman God has chosen for Isaac.

When a woman immediately appears who enthusiastically demonstrates these admirable qualities, and when she turns out to be a close relative of his master, the servant gives thanks and praise to God for making his journey successful. The sign the servant asked for wasn't arbitrary or capricious. It showed that God had already prepared the right kind of person to marry into Abraham's family.

⮑ Think about the situation in your life where you most need God's guidance and provision. If you feel comfortable doing so, tell your group what that situation is. Then have a time of prayer as a group. Ask God to "make things happen" ahead of each of you. Think of a way God could show you where he's already at work in your situation. Ask God to reveal his purposes for you through an appropriately chosen indication.

2 Rebekah will have a strong influence on the lives and destinies of Abraham's descendants. In this story, she first demonstrates the drive and initiative that will make her such a force in the future.

➲ Retell this story from Rebekah's perspective, starting from when she goes out to the town well to get water one evening. As Rebekah, why are you willing to leave with a stranger the next morning and travel a great distance from home to marry someone you've never met? (Different members of the group can tell different parts of the story, or one member can volunteer to tell the main story while others contribute ideas and details.)

3 Abraham lived nearly forty more years after Sarah died, and he had at least six more sons and seven grandsons by another wife, Keturah. But he was careful to make Isaac the undisputed legal heir of his possessions and of the covenant promises from God.

➲ Why do you think Abraham married Keturah after Sarah died? How can a widow or widower who remarries later in life do right by their new spouse and still honor the relationship they had with their first spouse?

ISAAC AND JACOB

THE DESCENDANTS OF ISHMAEL;
ISAAC GETS ESTABLISHED

Book of Genesis > Account of Ishmael
Book of Genesis > Account of Isaac > Isaac Story

INTRODUCTION

As the outline on page 11 illustrates, the book of Genesis alternates its focus between the particular family that God made a covenant with and other branches of the larger human family. Thus, after finishing the story of Abraham, Genesis looks briefly at Ishmael and his descendants, in the "account of Ishmael." It then returns its focus to the covenant family and tells the story of Isaac and his sons in much greater detail, in the "account of Isaac." This "account" will be mostly about the struggles and adventures of Isaac's son Jacob. But it begins with several brief stories about Isaac himself.

READING

Have different people read these scenes out loud:

The descendants of Ishmael ("This is the account of the family line of Abraham's son Ishmael . . .")

⭐ *The birth of Esau and Jacob* ("This is the account of the family line of Abraham's son Isaac . . .")

⭐ *Esau sells his birthright* ("The boys grew up, and Esau became a skillful hunter . . .")

⭐ *Isaac goes to live in Gerar* ("Now there was a famine in the land . . .")

⭐ *Isaac gets great wealth* ("Isaac planted crops in that land and the same year reaped a hundredfold . . .")

⭐ *Isaac's servants redig Abraham's wells* ("So Isaac moved away from there and encamped in the Valley of Gerar . . .")

⭐ *Abimelek makes a treaty with Isaac* (It begins, "From there he went up to Beersheba." It ends, "to this day the name of the town has been Beersheba.")

DISCUSSION

1 While the "account of Ishmael" is brief, it documents how God fulfilled two of the promises he'd made about Ishmael. God told Abraham he would make Ishmael "the father of twelve rulers." These tribal rulers are listed here.

God also told Hagar that Ishmael would live "over against his brothers" (literally in the Hebrew text). This suggests "hostility" (as in the TNIV translation), but it also implies geographical proximity: Ishmael and his family wouldn't go away and never be seen again. This account records that they settled just to the south and east of the land of Israel.

➲ What good things does God give to people whether or not they're in a direct covenant relationship with him?

2 Isaac and Rebekah's two sons begin a hostile rivalry before they're born. Jacob comes out of the womb grasping his brother's heel (the way someone might tackle another person from behind). Jacob becomes a calculating person and figures how to take advantage of his lusty, impetuous brother's live-for-the-moment attitude. Esau sells his birthright to Jacob to satisfy a momentary hunger.

⊃ God told Rebekah before her sons were born that "the older will serve the younger." Throughout the Bible we see God choosing younger brothers (for example, Jacob here and Isaac earlier) and other unlikely agents. He does this in order to fulfill his own plans in a way that's radically subversive of worldly power arrangements. But does God need Jacob to help him by cheating his unsuspecting brother like this? Where's the line between making ourselves available to be part of God's world-altering activity and taking matters into our own hands?

3 Isaac, facing a famine the way his father did years earlier, travels to Gerar and repeats the same mistake his father made twice before. He claims that Rebekah is his sister because he's afraid someone will kill him and take her away. This causes many problems for the unsuspecting king and his subjects.

⊃ Why do children tend to repeat their parents' mistakes? (Have you seen someone do this?) How can people become aware of destructive patterns in their families, realize that they're not inevitable, and begin to live in healthier ways?

4 While Isaac has some negative patterns to overcome, he's also received a great positive legacy from his father. It's both spiritual and material. God renews to Isaac all of the covenant promises he made to Abraham. And Isaac is able to reopen the wells Abraham's servants dug in this area to support his flocks and herds. While some of these are disputed, eventually Isaac secures two wells for himself, and he renews the peace treaty with Abimelek, the old ally of his father.

➲ What positive legacy has your family left you, materially and/or spiritually? What friends of your parents have been, or could be, a help to you in your own life?

JACOB STEALS THE FIRSTBORN'S BLESSING FROM ESAU

**Book of Genesis > Account of Isaac >
Jacob Story, Episode 1**

INTRODUCTION

The "account of Isaac" has summarized the major events of Isaac's life. It now moves to his later years and makes his son Jacob its main focus, because he will become the father of the twelve tribes of Israel.

Most of the story of Jacob's life, like the story of Abraham's life, is told in a nine-part chiasm built out of pairs of parallel episodes. The birth of Jacob's sons, the ancestors of the twelve tribes, is given the central place of highest importance. This chiasm is also quite lengthy, so we'll consider it over the course of the next four sessions. We'll begin in this session with the first episode.

A: Jacob deceives his father and steals Esau's blessing
  B: Jacob flees towards Harran and encounters God at Bethel
    C: Jacob arrives in Harran
      D: Laban deceives Jacob
        E: Jacob's children are born
      D: Jacob outwits Laban
    C: Jacob leaves Harran
  B: Jacob returns towards Canaan and encounters God again
A: Jacob returns Esau's blessing and they're reconciled

As this first episode opens, Issac is preparing to offer a deathbed blessing. This was a cherished custom of ancient times. Such blessings were considered powerful and prophetic. But there's something wrong with the picture: Isaac is preparing to bless only Esau, instead of both of his sons. Deathbed blessings were supposed to include the entire family. And how will God's word to Rebekah be fulfilled, "the older will serve the younger," if Isaac gives his older son the expected blessing of family supremacy?

READING

Have different people read the following passages in the story of Isaac's deathbed blessing. (But have the same person read the first and last passages.)

Esau marries two Hittite women. ("When Esau was forty years old . . .")

Isaac asks Esau to bring him a meal of wild game because he wants to bless him. ("When Isaac was old and his eyes were so weak . . .")

Rebekah instructs Jacob to pose as Esau in order to get his blessing. ("Now Rebekah was listening as Isaac spoke to his son Esau.")

Jacob brings a meal to Isaac and gets the firstborn's blessing. ("He went to his father and said, 'My father.'")

Esau brings in the game he's caught and the deception is discovered; he gets an inferior blessing. ("After Isaac finished blessing him, and Jacob had scarcely left . . .")

Rebekah warns Jacob to flee, and persuades Isaac to send him to Paddan Aram for a wife. ("When Rebekah was told what her older son Esau had said . . .")

Esau marries one of Ishmael's daughters. (It begins, "Now Esau learned that Isaac had blessed Jacob and had sent him to Paddan Aram . . ." It ends, ". . . daughter of Ishmael son of Abraham, in addition to the wives he already had.")

DISCUSSION

1 This is one of several examples of a deathbed blessing in the Bible. (We'll see Jacob himself offer deathbed blessings at the end of Genesis.) Children and grandchildren attached great importance to the words that were spoken about them on these occasions. They believed that they expressed their future destinies. Through Isaac's blessing, Jacob begins to inherit the covenant promises that were originally made to Abraham and more recently renewed to Isaac.

⮑ Have you been inspired by something an older relative predicted you could or would do? Do you think God sometimes reveals a person's destiny this way?

⮑ Can some family expectations and predictions become an obstacle to a person fulfilling God's purposes? Give an example.

2 In our last study we learned that "Isaac, who had a taste for wild game, loved Esau, but Rebekah loved Jacob." Now we see that Esau's relationship with his father had developed into an implicit arrangement of "indulge, and you'll be indulged." By catering to the gourmand in Isaac, Esau was able to steer him into permissive parenting.

While Abraham took the initiative to find Isaac a wife from his own clan by the time he was forty, Isaac apparently allowed Esau to choose any kind of wife he wanted for himself. When Esau turned forty, he married two Canaanite women. They were making life miserable for Rebekah. When she now discovers that her husband is about to bless only this impetuous, self-indulgent son and make him the new head of the family, she draws Jacob into a conspiracy of deception that successfully steals away the firstborn's blessing.

⊃ Hold a debate between these two positions: "Rebekah got in God's way here" vs. "Rebekah helped God." Group members can volunteer to be on a team that argues for either one of these positions, even if they're not personally convinced it's entirely correct. Other members can serve on a jury that decides which team wins the debate. Give each team time to prepare, five minutes to make its case, then two minutes to rebut the other team's arguments. Jury members can ask questions of each team before they deliberate and declare a winner.

JACOB FLEES TO HARRAN

**Book of Genesis > Account of Isaac >
Jacob Story, Episodes 2–5**

INTRODUCTION

In this session we'll consider the next four episodes in the chiasm that relates most of Jacob's life story:

B: Jacob flees towards Harran and encounters God at Bethel
   C: Jacob arrives in Harran
      D: Laban deceives Jacob
         E: Jacob's children are born

Rebekah knew that Jacob needed to get out of Esau's reach until his murderous rage subsided. She was able to persuade Isaac to let Jacob go to Harran by insisting he needed to find a wife from within his own clan. Jacob indeed marries within his clan and has many children. But once again God's purposes are accomplished through a maze of human rivalry and deception, and Jacob has to spend many years away from home.

READING

Have four people read each of these four episodes out loud. (They're set off from one another by white space in *The Books of The Bible*.)

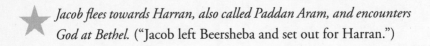
Jacob flees towards Harran, also called Paddan Aram, and encounters God at Bethel. ("Jacob left Beersheba and set out for Harran.")

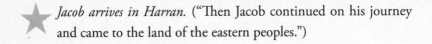
Jacob arrives in Harran. ("Then Jacob continued on his journey and came to the land of the eastern peoples.")

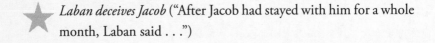
Laban deceives Jacob ("After Jacob had stayed with him for a whole month, Laban said . . .")

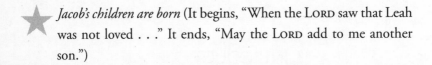
Jacob's children are born (It begins, "When the LORD saw that Leah was not loved . . ." It ends, "May the LORD add to me another son.")

DISCUSSION

1 Jacob, who was always "content to stay at home among the tents," must now wander out in the open, alone and without resources. He wonders where he'll even get "food to eat and clothes to wear." He's not able to find a place to stay the first night and lies down on the ground. But God appears to him in a dream and renews all of the promises he made to Abraham and Isaac. God assures Jacob specifically that he'll be with him on this journey, protect him, and bring him back home. In response, Jacob makes a vow: he'll become a devoted worshipper of this God if he'll see him safely through the dangerous and uncertain journey he's just beginning.

⮑ Have you ever found yourself in a situation like Jacob's, where you had to go to a new place on your own, without resources, not knowing what the future held? If you can, share with the group at least one example of how God watched over you and provided for you in this uncertain situation.

2 There are many similarities between the way Abraham's servant met Rebekah and the way Jacob now meets Rachel. God directs Jacob to just the right place; the future wife appears at a well; the young lady runs home and returns with Laban; he greets the visitor. But there are two important differences. Jacob's visit will last much longer than the servant's, and Jacob will shake up a lot of things while he's here.

He starts as soon as he arrives. Jacob was defying local conventions when he watered Laban's flocks. The ground rules seem to have been, "Nobody's flock gets watered until everybody arrives, we move the big stone together, and then it's first come, first served." Jacob points out how bad this approach is for the flocks: it denies them hours of good grazing. He also demonstrates that a single well-motivated shepherd can move the stone by himself. Thus he substitutes the principle of initiative for the privilege of first arrival. The clash of conventions has begun.

➲ Which position do you tend to agree with more?

a. Sometimes people get so used to doing things a certain way, it takes an outsider to help them see things objectively and do them more rationally and efficiently.

b. Settling on a certain way of doing things helps a group achieve a sense of cohesion and tradition. Those valuable things are threatened or destroyed when new people come along and challenge accepted ways.

➲ How can the community of Jesus' followers balance these two perspectives, so that it can be the guardian of the heritage of faith and also be open to new things that God wants to do?

3 There's another important difference between Jacob's arrival in Harran and the earlier visit of Abraham's servant. The servant brought lavish gifts for Rebekah and her family. Jacob arrives destitute. He can't pay the bride-price for Rachel, so he agrees to work for Laban for seven years. This is roughly the equivalent of the customary price, in labor.

At the end of these years, Jacob is eager to take his bride and return home. But Laban manages to substitute Leah for Rachel at the wedding feast. (How was this possible? Brides were veiled until the wedding night, and Laban may also have gotten Jacob drunk at the celebration, which is literally called a "drinking feast" in Hebrew.)

Jacob, the cheater, finds himself cheated. He stole Esau's firstborn blessing through manipulation and deception; now Laban justifies his own actions by appealing to *Leah's* rights as the firstborn. Laban also cites the local conventions Jacob has flouted: "It is not our custom here . . ."

Jacob will have to give Laban seven more years of labor to get the bride he really wants. (In this culture, he's allowed to have more than one wife.)

⊃ Do you agree or disagree with this statement: "The way we treat other people is the way other people will treat us—whether we want them to or not. The kind of person we are is the kind of person we'll get involved with—whether we want to or not."

4 Jacob becomes the father of a large family. His twelve sons will become the ancestors of the twelve tribes of Israel. But the family grows through the bitter rivalry of two sisters who are competing for their husband's affection by trying to outdo one another in bearing children. They each turn their female servants into secondary wives, just as Sarah did to Hagar. At one point they even negotiate a "stud fee" for Jacob!

Both Leah and Rachel claim that God is taking their side by giving them children. They express their claims in the names they give their sons. Once again Genesis depicts the purposes of God advancing through, or despite, human jockeying for advantage and supremacy.

⊃ Have the members of your group work together on four teams to tell this episode from the perspective of each of Jacob's wives: Leah, Rachel, Bilhah, and Zilpah. Emphasize how each woman would have thought God was at work on her own behalf, particularly in light of what's said about her children. Once each team has created its own version of the episode, have one team member read it out loud to the group.

JACOB FLEES BACK TOWARDS CANAAN

INTRODUCTION

In this session we'll consider two more episodes in the chiasm that relates most of Jacob's life story:

> D: Jacob outwits Laban
> C: Jacob leaves Harran

With his labor, Jacob has now paid the full bride-price for both of his wives, and he's eager to return home to Canaan. But Laban asks him to keep working for him. This could work out well for Jacob: He could begin to gather some wealth to support his family.

The two of them negotiate an agreement and Jacob develops a strong, healthy flock for himself. At the same time, Laban deals with Jacob so deceptively and dishonestly that he'd have nothing to show for these further years of work if it weren't for God's mercy and protection.

Eventually, sensing the resentment of Laban's family, Jacob secretly gathers his family and goods and makes a run for it. When Laban finds out, he takes a gang of his relatives and sets out in hot pursuit.

READING

Read these two episodes aloud like a play, taking the following parts:

 Jacob outwits Laban. (It begins, "After Rachel gave birth to Joseph, Jacob said to Laban . . .")
>   Narrator
>   Jacob
>   Laban

 Jacob flees from Laban. (It begins, "Jacob heard that Laban's sons were saying, 'Jacob has taken everything . . .'" It ends, "Early the next morning Laban kissed his grandchildren and his daughters and blessed them. Then he left and returned home.")
>   Narrator
>   Laban's sons
>   the LORD
>   Jacob
>   Rachel
>   Leah (in unison with Rachel)
>   Laban

DISCUSSION

1 Jacob showed a flair for productivity and efficiency from the time he first arrived in Harran. He explained to the local shepherds that they could give their flocks much more grazing time if they didn't water them so inefficiently. And through Jacob's talents, Laban's flocks grew large and strong. (As Jacob tells him, "The little you had before I came has increased greatly.")

Now Laban promises that every unusually colored animal will be Jacob's, and he gives him a free hand with the flock. Everything else being equal, a person of Jacob's talents could build a great flock under these conditions. Jacob does use ingenious means to get the animals to produce young that will belong to him.

But everything else isn't equal. Before Jacob has the chance to go through Laban's flock and claim his initial wages, Laban takes away all of the animals that should belong to him. And Jacob protests that afterwards Laban changed his wages "ten times"—constantly reinterpreting their agreement to suit his own interests. "If the God of my father . . . had not been with me," Jacob tells Laban, "you would surely have sent me away empty-handed."

➲ Have you ever had a boss or a business partner like Laban, who kept changing or reinterpreting the conditions of your work or pay? If a person can't get out of a situation like this, how can they experience God's protection and provision within the situation, as Jacob did?

2 Jacob hears Laban's sons complaining that he's stolen all of their family wealth. He fears that his in-laws may take away his goods by force. He's also afraid that Laban will try to take away his family. (Laban could appeal to the rule that slaves had to leave behind any wives they married and any children they had while in servitude. In other words, he could reinterpret their dealings once again and renege on the agreement to accept Jacob's labor in lieu of two bride prices.)

Rachel and Leah, for their part, see no point waiting around until their father is able to give them a dowry, since he's lost all of his wealth to their husband. So Jacob and his family take the only course they think will let them stay together and keep the wealth they've earned. At the busiest time of the year, when Laban is occupied and distracted by sheep-shearing, they run for their lives.

When Laban overtakes Jacob and his family, he says he would have sent them off "with joy and singing to the music of timbrels and harps." And he complains, "You didn't even let me kiss my grandchildren and my daughters good-by." Whether sincerely or not (he has to be on his best behavior after a stiff warning from God), Laban insists it would have been a good goodbye, and that Jacob has shamed himself by saying a bad goodbye instead.

➲ Are there times when it isn't safe or wise to try to say a good goodbye and we just need to get out of a situation? How can God help us get some healthy closure after a bad situation and even say a better goodbye than we might think possible, as Laban and Jacob do here when they make a peace treaty?

3 When Rachel steals her father's household gods, this may be a symbolic declaration of victory over him. (In the ancient world, victorious armies would carry away the gods of people they defeated.) These idols may also have been valuable, and Rachel might have been claiming them as her dowry. Or she may have wanted to keep worshipping them even when she returned with her husband to the land where the rest of his family worshipped "the God of Abraham and the Fear of Isaac."

Whatever her motives, Rachel shows she's just as deceptive as her father Laban, her aunt Rebekah, and her cousin and husband Jacob. She tricks Laban, and he doesn't find the gods in her tent.

➲ We've seen how the negative trait of deception runs deep in this family. But in these episodes we also see that this cunning can have a positive expression, in the talent for wise and effective management of resources. (In the next generation, Joseph will demonstrate this talent to an extraordinary degree.) Do you see a persistent negative trait appearing in several generations of your own family? What's the positive expression of this trait? How is God at work to lead you and your family members away from the negative expression into the positive one?

JACOB RETURNS TO THE LAND OF CANAAN

**Book of Genesis > Account of Isaac >
Jacob Story, Episodes 8 and 9**

INTRODUCTION

In this study we'll consider the last two episodes in the chiasm that relates most of Jacob's life story:

> B: Jacob returns towards Canaan and encounters God again
> A: Jacob returns Esau's blessing and they're reconciled

Jacob returns to the land of Canaan in obedience to God's instructions. But he won't be obeying God completely—he'll never be able to "go home" truly—until he rights the wrong he did that caused him to flee in the first place. Jacob needs to return the blessing he stole from his older brother Esau.

Most of the action in these episodes takes place by the Jabbok River. Jacob and his family are traveling west along the river back towards the land of Canaan. As you read the story, you can find the Jabbok River, Mahanaim, Peniel and Sukkoth on the map for this session.

READING

Have five people read these two episodes out loud like a play:

Jacob returns towards Canaan and encounters God again (beginning, "Jacob also went on his way, and the angels of God met him").
    Narrator
    Jacob
    messengers
    the man who wrestles with Jacob

Jacob returns Esau's blessing and they're reconciled. (This episode begins, "Jacob looked up and there was Esau . . ." It ends, "That is why the place is called Sukkoth.")
    Narrator
    Jacob
    Esau

DISCUSSION

1 When Jacob says, "Please accept the *present* that was brought to you," this isn't the same word that's translated "gift" in the rest of the story. It's actually the word *blessing*. Jacob is insisting that Esau receive back the blessing he stole from him.

Jacob makes restitution in tangible ways. Isaac's blessing had included agricultural abundance; Jacob gives Esau large herds and flocks. Isaac blessed Jacob by saying, "May the sons of your mother bow down to you." Now Jacob, his wives, and their children all bow down to Esau. Isaac said to Esau, "I have made [Jacob] lord over you." Now Jacob addresses Esau as "my lord" and speaks of himself as Esau's "servant." Jacob is able to put things back to where they would have been if he'd never stolen the blessing.

⮑ Have you (or has someone you know) had the chance to make or receive restitution like this? If so, share the story if you can.

JACOB'S RETURN TO CANAAN

Damascus

▲ Mt. Hermon

ARAM

• Tyre

PHOENICIA

Mediterranean
Sea

Sea of Galilee

▲ Mt. Carmel

Yarmuk River

ISRAEL

Jordan River

Jacob's return journey
from Paddan-Aram

Peniel

Mahanaim

Shechem

Sukkoth

Jabbok River

Jarkon River

Bethel

Ai

AMMON

Jacob's travels in
the land of Canaan

Jericho

Ashdod

Ekron

JERUSALEM

Bethlehem

Gath

JUDAH

Ashkelon

PHILISTIA

Dead
Sea

Gaza

Hebron

Arnon River

Gerar

MOAB

Beersheba

0   20 Mi

20 Km

Zered River

NEGEV

EDOM

2 When Jacob hears that Esau is coming to meet him with four hundred men, he prays to God for protection and deliverance. His prayer is the longest one recorded in the Bible to this point. It provides a model for our own prayers by including a variety of appropriate elements.

➲ Match each of the elements in the left-hand column below with the specific phrases in Jacob's prayer, in the right-hand column, that express them:

a. The person praying notes how they've obeyed God's directions to this point.	O God of my father Abraham, God of my father Isaac, LORD, you who said to me, "Go back to your country and your relatives, and I will make you prosper,"
b. A promise from God is recalled that gives confidence a request will be granted.	I am unworthy of all the kindness and faithfulness you have shown your servant. I had only my staff when I crossed this Jordan, but now I have become two camps.
c. God's past blessings are acknowledged with thanksgiving and humility.	
d. God is addressed by names and titles appropriate to the subject of the prayer.	Save me, I pray, from the hand of my brother Esau, for I am afraid he will come and attack me, and also the mothers with their children.
e. Direct petition is made for a specific need or concern.	But you have said, "I will surely make you prosper and will make your descendants like the sand of the sea, which cannot be counted."

3 The "man" who wrestles with Jacob is a figure much like the "angel of the LORD" who's appeared in Genesis before. He represents God on earth, in his dealings with a particular individual. The wrestling match is a symbolic reenactment of how Jacob has "struggled with God and with human beings" and overcome.

By facing and meeting great trials, Jacob has deepened his character and developed strength and tenacity. These are illustrated in the demand he makes: "I won't let you go unless you bless me!"

In order to bless Jacob, the "man" has to ask his name. This provides the occasion for Jacob to be given a new name, just as Abraham and Sarah were given new names to express their deepening covenant relationship with God. Jacob, the "heel grasper," will now be known as "Israel," the one who "wrestles with God." He'll have God's direct blessing, pronounced by this representative, rather than a blessing stolen from his older brother.

Jacob's experience here at Peniel is a divine encounter very similar to his experience at Bethel twenty years earlier. Then he said, "This is none other than the house of God." Now he says, "I saw God face to face." The chance to relive an earlier experience shows how much Jacob has changed and grown over the years.

⊃ Think of a meaningful experience you had some years ago. Picture the person you are today stepping into that experience. How do you act and respond differently? How have the experiences that God has brought into your life made you change and grow?

4 When Jacob leaves Canaan, the sun sets: "He stopped for the night because the sun had set." Now, as Jacob returns to Canaan, the sun rises: "The sun rose above him as he passed Peniel." The sun is never mentioned in between. This artistic touch illustrates that a long, dark period of difficult struggles in Jacob's life has at last come to an end.

⊃ Have you gone through a "dark night" in your life and eventually come out of it into a "new day"? What encouragement would you offer to someone who might still be struggling in a "dark night"?

JACOB'S FAMILY BACK IN CANAAN

**Book of Genesis > Account of Isaac >
Jacob Story, Final Episodes**

INTRODUCTION

The "account of Isaac" concludes by describing what happens to Jacob and his family once they return to Canaan. They think they've settled safely back in the land, near the city of Shechem. But soon an outrageous crime is committed against them. A man who's also named Shechem, the son of a local ruler, rapes Jacob's daughter Dinah. Even though he then tries to make amends by marrying her, her brothers take such violent revenge that it's no longer safe for Jacob's family to stay in this area. They move south in three stages, from Shechem to Bethel, then to Bethlehem, and finally to Hebron, where they rejoin Jacob's father, the aged patriarch Isaac. The "account of Isaac" closes by describing his death and burial.

READING

Have six people read, in parts, the story of what happened to Jacob's family by the city of Shechem. (It begins, "After Jacob came from Paddam Aram, he arrived safely at the city of Shechem . . .")

Narrator

Shechem

Hamor
Simeon and Levi (Jacob's sons)
Jacob

Then have three people read the descriptions of the three stages of Jacob's family's journey from Shechem to Hebron:

 From Shechem to Bethel. ("Then God said to Jacob, 'Go up to Bethel . . .'")

 From Bethel to Ephrath (Bethlehem). ("Then they moved on from Bethel.")

 From Ephrath to Hebron. (It begins, "Israel moved on again and pitched his tent beyond Migdal Eder." It ends, "And his sons Esau and Jacob buried him.")

You can follow their progress on this journey by looking at the map that accompanies session 20.

DISCUSSION

1 As a relatively small band of people living in foreign territory, Jacob's family is vulnerable to crimes of violence and violation. Rapists like Shechem are trying to assert their dominance over their victims. As the privileged member of the local ruler's family, Shechem thinks he's entitled to have his way with Dinah when she innocently goes out to make friends with the other women in the area.

But he then falls in love with her and wants to marry her. He detains her in his house and goes to tell her family he'll pay any bride-price they name. Dinah's father Jacob, perhaps feeling the helplessness of his position, does nothing about the crime while his sons are out with their flocks. But when they return, they meet with Shechem and his father Hamor and, through an elaborate deception, render them defenseless.

The Shechemites fall for the ruse completely because of their greed: they say to one another, "Won't their livestock, their property and all their other animals become ours?" Instead, Simeon and Levi slaughter the incapacitated Shechemites and bring Dinah back. Jacob's sons take all of their possessions and carry off their wives. It's retributive justice: the violent suffer violence, and lose exactly what they expected to gain. But the vengeance is also horribly disproportionate: all the men of the city die because of one man's crime.

➲ If you have artists in your group, have them retell this story visually by drawing Dinah's face when she first went out to meet the other women; when she was detained in Shechem's house; and after she was brought back by her brothers. Have the artists show their drawings and have the group share their observations about them.

➲ Should Dinah's family have responded in some different way to what happened to her? Share your thoughts about each of the following possibilities:

    a. Let Shechem marry Dinah, but make him pay a punitive bride-price.

    b. Send several of Dinah's brothers to rescue her secretly from Shechem's house while the rest of the family moves to a safer location.

    c. Take Shechem to the gate of his city, where legal matters are settled, and bring a charge of rape against him.

    d. Pass judgment on Shechem within the family itself and designate an avenger to carry out whatever sentence the family decides on.

2 Dinah was raped by an "outsider," but Bilhah was violated by a member of her own family. Jacob will eventually punish Reuben by taking away his firstborn blessing. This, as we've seen, was a significant loss of status and privilege. But no one angrily and publicly demands retribution, as they did for Dinah. Reuben never comes forward and offers to make things right, as Shechem did. Even in the narrative the crime is passed over in near-silence.

➲ Based on what you've learned so far in Genesis from the experience of other women who were mistreated, how would you say God responds to what happens to Bilhah? What do you make of this? How would you offer spiritual comfort to those who've experienced "secret" abuse from a family member?

➲ Pray together as a group for an end to crimes of sexual violence, for the healing and restoration of those who've suffered from these crimes, and for the correction of those who've committed them.

JOSEPH AND HIS BROTHERS

INTO THE NEXT GENERATION:
THE LEGACIES OF ESAU AND JACOB

Book of Genesis > Account of Esau (as head of a family)
Book of Genesis > Account of Esau
**   (as the ancestor of a nation)**
Book of Genesis > Account of Jacob >
Joseph Story begins

INTRODUCTION

As the book of Genesis moves into the next generation after the death of Isaac, it follows its characteristic pattern by first focusing briefly on Esau's descendants, then telling the story of Jacob's descendants in much greater detail.

There are actually two "accounts" of Esau. The first considers him as the head of one branch of the family descended from Abraham. But when Esau moves out of the land where God told Abraham and Isaac to live, and he and his offspring intermarry with the descendants of Seir, they become a separate nation, Edom. The second "account" of Esau thus describes him as the ancestor of the Edomites.

The "account of Jacob" is the last and longest account in the book of Genesis. It begins here with a description of how the favoritism and deception that caused so much trouble for Isaac's family were repeated in the next generation, with even more destructive results.

READING

Have someone read the first "account of Esau" out loud. Then give your group members a few minutes to read silently through the second "account of Esau," noting how it documents three things: (1) Esau's grandsons by his first two wives, and his sons by his third wife, become local chiefs; (2) Esau's family intermarries with the clan of Seir the Horite; (3) Edom develops into a separate kingdom from Israel. This is a further fulfillment of Isaac's blessing on Esau: "You will serve your brother. But when you grow restless, you will throw off his yoke from off your neck."

Then read the story of Joseph and his brothers out loud like a play. (It begins, "Jacob lived in the land where his father had stayed, the land of Canaan." It ends, "the Midianites sold Joseph in Egypt to Potiphar, one of Pharaoh's officials, the captain of the guard.")

Narrator

Joseph

Jacob (Joseph's father)

the man from Shechem

Reuben

Judah (Have the actors who play Reuben and Judah also speak the part of "his brothers.")

DISCUSSION

1 The dreams Joseph has as a young man suggest that he has a special destiny in life. Even though he has ten older brothers, he'll become the family leader. But do these dreams really come from God? They do have a significant character: one takes place on earth, while the other takes place in the heavens, as if they bore double witness to a divine purpose for Joseph's life.

But Joseph's brothers see matters differently. Infuriated that their little brother thinks he's going to rule over them, they suggest they can settle the matter very simply: "Let's kill him . . . Then we'll see what comes of his dreams."

◔ Have you ever had any actual dreams that you believe express something about God's purposes for your life? Have you ever reached a place where your "dreams" (actual or figurative) seemed to have hit a "dead end," only to live on unexpectedly? What's the current status of your dreams?

◔ Pray for one another, that you'll understand the dreams God wants you to have for your lives, and that you'll see them realized in ways you couldn't even imagine now.

2 Jacob blatantly favors Joseph above his other sons, just as his own father Isaac favored Esau. He has Joseph, even as a young man, supervise and report on his older half-brothers, the sons of Bilhah and Zilpah.

Jacob also makes Joseph a distinctive garment that signifies superior status. This garment has traditionally been known as a "coat of many colors" (or, in the theater, as an "amazing technicolor dreamcoat"). It's more likely, however, that this was actually a "long-sleeved coat," that is, a "white-collar" outfit for a supervisor who wasn't expected to get his hands dirty. Jacob now sends Joseph out to observe and report on all of his brothers.

◔ Have you ever been in a situation where a parent, teacher, or employer showed favoritism to you or someone else? How did this affect relationships within the family, class, or workplace? Is favoritism a sin?

◔ Retell the story of Joseph's visit to his brothers at Dothan from Judah's perspective. Have Judah tell a friend about what he believes he's gotten away with, and not hold back any details about what he did or what he was thinking, since he has no fear of being caught.

JUDAH AND TAMAR

INTRODUCTION

While the "account of Jacob" primarily tells the story of Joseph's life, its larger purpose is to describe how a nation of twelve tribes began to develop from Jacob's family of twelve sons. And so the account temporarily leaves off the story of Joseph to explain how the tribe of Judah, which became one of the largest and most powerful in Israel, first began to grow. This story also contributes to the unfolding portrait of Judah himself. He's already played a key role in the narrative by persuading his brothers to sell Joseph into slavery. He'll have further key roles to play later in the story. The preceding episode has offered a broad character sketch of Judah; here more details are filled in and we see Judah's character become deeper and more complex. Here we also meet Tamar, another of the resourceful (in fact, audacious) women in Genesis who keep steering Abraham's family towards its divinely appointed destiny, by means we can often only wonder at.

READING

Read the story of Judah and Tamar out loud like a play. (It begins, "At that time, Judah left his brothers . . ." It ends, "he was given the name Zerah.")

If this story were a movie, it would not be rated "G," so choose a narrator and actors who are comfortable with "mature subject matter."

Narrator
Judah
Tamar
Hirah the Adullamite
men of Enaim

DISCUSSION

1 In this culture, women were dependent on male relatives for support and protection. If a husband died and left no children, his brother was expected to marry his widow and give her children of her own.

After Er dies, Onan pretends he is trying to do this for Tamar. But he's actually cruelly and deceptively depriving her of children. When God strikes Onan dead for this, Judah promises Tamar she can marry his remaining son Shelah when he's old enough. But Judah doesn't honor this promise. Tamar finally gets her late husband's family to fulfill its obligation to her by reading Judah's character shrewdly, posing as a prostitute, intercepting him on a journey, and soliciting sex with him.

⊃ Judah holds all of the legal and cultural power here. Nevertheless, Tamar defeats him by using a different power. Where in our own culture do we see a message being sent to women that they can (or should, or must) use sex or sexuality to get what they need and want? How can women be encouraged to acquire other forms of power? What different powers might Tamar have drawn upon to influence Judah to do the right thing?

⊃ How can men be encouraged to include women in their own circles of power? How could Judah have used his legal and cultural power to provide for Tamar—to empower her in new ways?

2 Despite the measures that Tamar uses, Judah declares that she was actually more justified than he was. By failing to provide for her needs as a widow, he did worse to her than she did to his family by being unfaithful to Shelah, her supposed fiancé. God seems to agree that it's a very serious thing to deprive a widow of support, since he strikes Onan dead as punishment for denying children to Tamar. This is an unusual measure that indicates a very serious sin. (God also strikes Er dead for some unnamed "wickedness.")

○ Are sexual sins less serious in God's eyes than sins of injustice? Explain your view.

3 Tamar's children Perez and Zerah were born under circumstances their culture considered shameful. They were conceived through prostitution, adultery, and incest (sexual relations between a man and his daughter-in-law). Nevertheless, they became the ancestors of the largest and most powerful tribe in Israel. Their later distinguished descendants included King David and Jesus Christ. God therefore had a vital purpose for bringing these children into the world, a purpose that was unaffected by the circumstances of their birth.

○ What birth circumstances does your own culture attach shame to? Children aren't at all responsible for the circumstances of their own birth, so how can they be set free from any feelings of shame they might carry about it?

4 Judah had callously encouraged his brothers to sell Joseph into slavery, asking, "What will we gain if we kill him?" (By selling him as a slave, they each got the equivalent of three months' wages.)

In this episode he similarly seems to lack any conscience. While his father and grandfather had been careful not to marry Canaanite women, Judah marries one himself and apparently gets a Canaanite wife (Tamar) for his first son as well. He casually and commercially has sex with a woman he thinks is a prostitute. And when he learns that his widowed daughter-in-law, who's now engaged to his youngest son, has become pregnant by some other man, he insists on a most severe penalty: burning her alive.

But when Tamar produces the personal tokens Judah gave her as a guarantee of payment, proving that he's the "other man," he's finally conscience-stricken. His declaration, "She is more righteous than I," is actually a legal verdict. It means, "She's more in the right, and I'm more in the wrong, in this legal matter."

⮕ Judah could have refused to acknowledge that the tokens were his, and tried to continue blaming Tamar for everything. Why do you think Judah acknowledges his own guilt at this point? Is he genuinely taking responsibility, or does he just think he can't get away with what he's done? Has something broken through and awakened his conscience? If so, what?

JOSEPH AS A SLAVE AND A PRISONER

**Book of Genesis > Account of Jacob >
Joseph Story continues**

INTRODUCTION

The account of Jacob now returns to the story of Joseph and describes what happened to him after he was brought into Egypt.

READING

Have someone read aloud what happened to Joseph while he was a slave in Potiphar's house. (This episode begins, "Now Joseph had been taken down to Egypt.")

Then have someone read how Joseph interpreted the cupbearer and baker's dreams after he was put in prison. (This episode begins, "Some time later, the cupbearer and the baker of the king of Egypt offended their master . . ." It ends, "The chief cupbearer, however, did not remember Joseph; he forgot him.")

DISCUSSION

1 Joseph has remarkable administrative ability, and because "the LORD is with him" in slavery and in prison, everything he does prospers.

Earlier his father made him supervisor of the family flocks. Now Potiphar and the prison warden entrust their entire operations to him, without a care. Eventually Joseph will be given significantly greater responsibilities. But first God deepens and develops his character through these experiences.

As a slave and a prisoner, Joseph has no formal power or authority to make people follow his instructions. Instead, he has to rely on his own character and ability, so these are developed with every passing day. Later, when he has a higher position, he will be able to use the power and authority that come with it much more effectively because of his deepened character and sharpened ability.

⤳ Name one of the most difficult jobs you've ever done. What made it so difficult? Looking back on the experience now, can you identify how it may have strengthened your character and ability, and equipped you better to do something significant in the future?

2 As we saw in session 23, Tamar recognized that Judah wouldn't be able to resist falling into a trap that was baited with sexual desire. Joseph, on the other hand, is able to resist Potiphar's wife's repeated invitations to have an affair with her.

⤳ How was Joseph able to resist this temptation? What might it have meant to him to have an affair with Potiphar's wife? How might Joseph have rationalized doing this?

⤳ Why would the wife of a court official want to have an affair with a household slave? What would it have meant to her to have Joseph as a lover?

⤳ What do you think was the first thing Joseph said to God after he was thrown in prison?

3 The cupbearer and baker each have dreams that accurately predict the future. God enables Joseph to interpret the dreams and explain their meaning.

⊃ Do you think God still speaks to people through dreams today? Do you know someone who's had a dream that seemed to predict the future? Do you know anyone who's able to interpret dreams? How do they account for this ability? Is it dangerous to rely on dreams as expressions of God's plans and purposes?

JOSEPH INTERPRETS PHARAOH'S DREAM AND BECOMES A RULER OF EGYPT

INTRODUCTION

There are three pairs of dreams in the story of Joseph's life. As a young man, he had two dreams about his destiny to become a family leader. When Joseph was put in prison, he interpreted the cupbearer and baker's dreams about their own futures. And now Joseph is called upon to interpret a pair of dreams that Pharaoh has about what lies in store for Egypt. When Joseph does this, his own dreams for himself are finally fulfilled.

READING

Read the story of how Joseph interpreted Pharaoh's dreams and prepared Egypt to face seven years of famine. (It begins, "When two full years had passed . . ." It ends, "And all the world came to Egypt to buy grain from Joseph, because the famine was severe everywhere.") Have people take these parts:

> Narrator
>
> cupbearer
>
> Pharaoh
>
> Joseph

DISCUSSION

1 Earlier we saw how a sunset and sunrise marked the beginning and ending of the "darkness" period in Jacob's life. What Joseph calls the "suffering" period in his own life is marked similarly by a narrative detail.

His childhood of optimism and privilege comes to an abrupt end when his brothers throw him in a "cistern" (literally a "pit"). Now, as he begins a new stage of life marked by maturity and responsibility, Genesis tells us that he's brought out of a "dungeon" (once again, literally a "pit"—not the word for "prison" used elsewhere in the story). It's as if Joseph has been in the pit his brothers threw him into for the past thirteen years and is finally emerging.

⊃ Have people do this exercise individually first, then share their answers with the rest of the group: Draw a "timeline" of your life, dividing it into its major significant periods. Think about whether a repeated event or experience marks the boundaries of one or more of these periods. Could this represent God's "fingerprints" as he crafts your life?

2 The cupbearer had met Joseph and discovered his God-given ability to interpret dreams. Now he was in the right place at the right time to introduce Joseph to Pharaoh.

⊃ Can you name someone you met earlier in life who later proved to be a "divine contact" by connecting you with a person or organization you were able to work with to fulfill an important purpose?

3 At the end of these episodes Joseph has a new identity. He's no longer "that Hebrew slave," as Potiphar's wife described him. He's now Zaphenath-Paneah, a powerful royal official who's married into an elite priestly family. When he starts a family of his own, he names his first son "Manasseh" ("forgetting") and says, "God has made me forget . . . all my father's household." Even though he told the cupbearer in prison he'd been "forcibly carried off from the land of the Hebrews" (implying he should really be allowed to return there), now he seems to think of himself as an Egyptian who belongs in this country.

⮑ Have the members of your group arrange themselves in a line based on how different their current social identity is from their original one. Use factors like these to measure change in identity: having a different name; living in another region or country; speaking a new language; following a different religion; becoming part of another family; following a different profession from either parent; other factors that are significant for people in your group. Give people one "point" for each factor. Put the person with the highest total on one end, and the person with the lowest total on the other end. Using this as a scale, have the other members place themselves at the appropriate spot along the line. Then have group members describe, if they can, how the change, or lack of change, in their identity has made them more effective in the work God has given them to do.

JOSEPH'S BROTHERS COME TO BUY GRAIN

**Book of Genesis > Account of Jacob >
Joseph Story continues**

INTRODUCTION

The "account of Jacob" now brings the rest of Jacob's family back into the picture. While Joseph has made sure there's enough food in Egypt, there's famine in "all the other lands." How will the rest of his family survive the famine in Canaan so they can grow into a nation, as God has promised? If his brothers go to Egypt to buy food from Joseph, will he sell it to them, or will he see this as the perfect opportunity to take revenge? Can there be forgiveness and reconciliation between Joseph and his brothers, as there was between Jacob and Esau? These questions begin to be answered as Joseph's brothers make a first journey down to Egypt. As the climax of the Joseph story approaches, the narrative is shaped in increasingly artful ways. The events of this first journey are related as a chiasm:

A: Jacob sends Joseph's brothers to buy grain
   B: They travel to Egypt
      C: They meet with Joseph
      C: They meet with Joseph again
   B: They travel back to Canaan
A: Joseph's brothers report back to Jacob

READING

Have three members of your group read the story of Joseph's brothers' first journey to Egypt. Assign a letter from A to C to each speaker, and have them read the episodes identified by that letter in the diagram above. The episodes begin with these phrases:

A. "When Jacob learned that there was grain in Egypt . . ."

B. "Then ten of Joseph's brothers went down to buy grain from Egypt."

C. "Now Joseph was the governor of the land . . ."

C. "On the third day Joseph said to them . . ."

B. "Joseph gave orders to fill their bags with grain . . ."

A. "When they came to their father Jacob in the land of Canaan . . ."

DISCUSSION

1 Joseph has settled comfortably into a new life in Egypt, concluding, "God has made me forget all my trouble and all my father's household." But now his brothers suddenly appear before him. He recognizes them and "remembers his dreams about them" as they bow down to him. He also notices something wrong with the picture: his full brother Benjamin is missing. Have his half-brothers disposed of him out of jealousy, too?

Joseph doesn't tell his brothers right away who he is. Instead, he accuses them falsely, questions them closely and discovers Benjamin is alive, and throws them into prison before he finally lets them buy food and leave, keeping one of them as a hostage.

⮑ Why do you think Joseph treats his brothers this way? Rank the following possible motives: which do you think was Joseph's most important motive, which was the next most important, and so on? Would any of these motives justify what he does?

a. "This is payback time. Now my brothers are going to find out how it feels to be falsely accused and lose your freedom!"

b. "Thank God that Benjamin is alive and safe, at least for now. But I've got to get him out of my half-brothers' clutches, and I can't let them know what I'm doing."

c. "Before attempting any reconciliation, I need to find out whether they feel remorse for what they did to me. If I really turn up the heat, what they're feeling inside will come out."

d. Another possible motive you can think of.

2 In this episode we get more information about what happened when Joseph's brothers threw him into a pit. We learn that there was some length of time when they "saw how distressed he was" as he "pleaded with us for his life," but they still "would not listen." In fact, according to the first account, as he suffered hunger and thirst, they were sitting around eating a meal—perhaps some special foods Joseph himself had brought to them from their father.

➲ To appreciate what Joseph has to overcome if he's to forgive his brothers, re-create what he and his brothers may have said to one another when Joseph was in the pit. What arguments would Joseph have used as he pleaded for his life? What cruel, sarcastic things might his brothers have said in return, now that they had this favored, resented younger brother in their power? Sample dialogue:

Joseph: Please, please help me! It's so cold and dark in this pit!

Brother: You're cold? Just put on your long-sleeved coat. Oh yes, we've got it up here, don't we? (Laughter.)

Another brother: You say it's dark down there? I hear you can see the stars from the bottom of a well. Are they still bowing down to you?

Carry the dialogue up to the point where the brothers sell Joseph into slavery. Then have several members of your group act it out. What's the emotional impact?

JOSEPH'S BROTHERS RETURN WITH BENJAMIN

**Book of Genesis > Account of Jacob >
Joseph Story continues**

This session involves a much longer reading than usual. The next is shorter. So if you don't finish this session in one meeting, you may decide to finish it in your next meeting along with session 28.

INTRODUCTION

Eventually Joseph's brothers have to go back to Egypt to buy more food. Jacob allows them to bring Benjamin with them, since this is the only way the family can stay alive. This second journey provides the climax of the Joseph story. Like the first journey, it's arranged as a chiasm. But there's a significant difference. The second journey has an additional element:

A: Jacob agrees to let Joseph's brothers return to Egypt with Benjamin
  B: They arrive; conversation with Joseph's steward
    C: They meet with Joseph
      D: They start home, but are overtaken and arrested
    C: They're taken to meet with Joseph again
  B: They leave Egypt; conversation with Pharaoh
A: They return to Canaan and report to Jacob

Hebrew listeners would recognize this chiasm taking shape. When they felt the action turning around as the brothers were arrested and then brought back to Joseph, their literary sensibilities would suggest that this arrest was the central element of the story. Does this mean Joseph ultimately decided to take revenge, rather than forgive? Did he detain Benjamin in Egypt and send the others back to face their father's retribution? The literary structure creates suspense about what Joseph will do when his brothers are brought back to him, and this makes the events of that scene even more dramatic. Enjoy the masterful storytelling, and listen in as Joseph's brothers face him once again . . .

READING

Have four members of your group read the story of Joseph's brothers' second journey to Egypt. Assign a letter from A to D to each speaker and have them read the episodes identified by that letter in the diagram above. The episodes begin with these phrases:

A. "Now the famine was still severe in the land."

B. "So the men took the gifts and double the amount of silver . . ."

C. "When Joseph came home, they presented to him the gifts they had brought . . ."

D. "Now Joseph gave these instructions to the steward of his house."

C. "Joseph was still in the house when Judah and his brothers came in."

B. "When the news reached Pharaoh's palace that Joseph's brothers had come . . ."

A. "So they went up out of Egypt and came to their father Jacob . . ." (End with Jacob saying, "I will go and see him before I die.")

DISCUSSION

1 When Joseph first saw his brothers after many years, on their first trip to Egypt, he hid his identity and pursued an elaborate ruse, forcing them to go back to Canaan for Benjamin. When he now sees them again, on this second trip, he begins by speaking reassuring words to them. But then he alternates gracious hospitality with harsh accusations and trumped-up charges. Finally, however, Joseph determines that his brothers have had a genuine change of heart, and that it's safe to express forgiveness and pursue reconciliation with them.

⮕ What things did Joseph's brothers say and do on their two visits to Egypt that showed Joseph they were sorry for what they'd done to him? How could he tell they would now relate differently to him and Benjamin?

⮕ What are some of the general signs that it may be safe to begin pursuing reconciliation with someone who's hurt you? On the other hand, what are the signs that they'd only hurt you again if you gave them the opportunity?

⮕ Can you genuinely forgive another person without expressing that forgiveness to them directly, in person? Can you forgive a person without pursuing reconciliation with them, if you don't think that would be safe yet? Explain.

2 Judah is the oldest of Jacob's sons who's still in good standing with him. (This will be confirmed shortly when Jacob extends and withholds his deathbed blessings.) So when the family has to buy food again, Judah steps up to a position of leadership and promises his father he'll guarantee Benjamin's safety so the brothers can return to Egypt.

In order to keep this promise once they arrive, Judah offers personally to become Joseph's slave. This gesture, from the brother who originally suggested selling him into slavery, moves Joseph so profoundly that he reveals his identity and expresses his forgiveness.

➲ Judah provides critical leadership here by being responsible and self-sacrificing. Earlier, however, he was impetuous and self-indulgent. He mistreated both Joseph and Tamar. Is Judah a "good character" or a "bad character" in Genesis? Defend your answer.

3 Joseph ultimately says to his brothers, "Do not be angry with yourselves for selling me here, because it was to save lives that God sent me ahead of you . . . So then, it was not you who sent me here, but God." Throughout his time in Egypt, Joseph has shown a remarkable awareness of God's presence and activity. Now he's able to see God's presence, activity, and purposes even in the worst thing that ever happened to him.

➲ Have you been able to look back on a difficult experience and see how God was at work for good in it, for you and for others around you? Share your story with the group if you feel comfortable doing so.

➲ How do you think Joseph was able to remain so aware of God in the midst of suffering, setbacks, and temptation? The narrator in Genesis tells us that "the LORD was with Joseph" as a slave, and again that "the LORD was with Joseph" in prison. How did Joseph know that God was with him?

JACOB'S FAMILY MOVES TO EGYPT

**Book of Genesis > Account of Jacob >
Joseph Story continues**

INTRODUCTION

Even though God told Abraham, Isaac, and Jacob to live in the land of Canaan, Jacob now moves his entire family down to Egypt so that Joseph can provide for them during the famine. God reassures Jacob that he'll be with him there and bless him. Jacob and his extended family settle in the land of Goshen, with Pharaoh's blessing. Then Joseph acquires all of the money, livestock, and land in Egypt for Pharaoh and turns all the people into Pharaoh's slaves. Has the family been trapped there?

READING

Have someone read aloud the descriptions of Jacob's vision at Beersheba and his family's journey from Beersheba to Egypt. ("So Israel set out with all that was his, and when he reached Beersheba . . .")

Then have five people read the list of Jacob's descendants. ("These are the names of the sons of Israel . . .") Have one person read the opening and conclusion, and have the others each read one of the four parts that describe the offspring of Leah, Zilpah, Rachel, and Bilhah. (Each of the parts ends with a summary that names one of these women.)

Have someone read the description of how Jacob's family settled in Egypt. ("Now Jacob sent Judah ahead of him to Joseph . . .")

Finally, have someone read how Joseph acquired all of the goods in Egypt for Pharaoh. ("There was no food, however, in the whole region because the famine was severe . . . They acquired property there and were fruitful and increased greatly in number.")

DISCUSSION

1 When Jacob first left the land of Canaan as a young man, God appeared to him in a dream at Bethel and promised, "I am with you and will watch over you wherever you go, and I will bring you back to this land." Now, near the end of his life, Jacob has to leave Canaan again. God appears to him in a vision at Beersheba, says "do not be afraid," and promises, "I will go down to Egypt with you, and I will surely bring you back again."

⮑ Which do you think is harder: to "leave home" for the first time as a young person, or to leave what has become your "home" as an older person? Do you know an older person who has shown faith and courage by moving away from "home" late in life? What circumstances made this move necessary or advisable? What, if anything, did the person say about how they believed God would take care of them?

2 The book of Genesis tells us here, "All those who went to Egypt with Jacob . . . numbered sixty-six persons." But the group actually numbered 65 persons, since Joseph was already in Egypt, and had been there for twenty years. To make the numbers add up, we have to consider that Joseph was somehow going "with" the rest of the family when, as he puts it, God "sent him ahead" so many years earlier. Genesis considers his trip to Egypt as a slave part of the larger group's journey because he prepared the way as an advance agent.

⮑ Can you see some ways in which God may have "sent" you into your current situation for the sake of others who have followed you into it?

⮑ Have you benefited from the help of "advance agents" yourself? (Think back over some of the places where you've lived, worked, or studied. Had God already put people in place there whose help and influence were vital to you?)

3 It may seem unjust that Joseph doesn't simply give food to the people who are suffering from this famine. Instead, he makes them pay for it with all of their money, livestock, and land, and ultimately with their freedom.

But the situation may not actually be as unjust as it seems. It was common in the ancient world for a person who fell on hard times to mortgage valuable possessions such as land or livestock until they could get back on their feet again. Family members would feel responsible to pay off the debts of a relative who'd mortgaged assets like this, so these were often short-term arrangements. A person could even mortgage their own labor and agree to become someone else's servant for a time. Someone in financial difficulty would be grateful to anyone who helped them in return for their assets or labor. Thus the Egyptians say to Joseph, "You have saved our lives!"

If there is a problem here, it's because this mortgaging takes place on a nationwide scale, and the creditor is an absolute ruler. It's one thing for an individual to mortgage an asset to a sympathetic friend or relative in a climate of general prosperity. It's quite another thing for an entire population to turn their land, livestock and labor over to the nation's ruler. The state now has a monopoly on the means of production, and no one can regain their financial independence.

⮑ Are there some things that individuals can do that large entities such as government and corporations shouldn't be allowed to do, because their actions have much greater effects? Do these large entities need to be held to stricter standards? Is there a difference between "private morality" and "corporate morality"?

⮕ As a group, agree on a service project you can do together to help overcome hunger in your own community, or identify an organization you can make a group donation to that's providing relief to a part of the world affected by hunger.

JACOB'S DEATHBED BLESSINGS

**Book of Genesis > Account of Jacob >
Joseph Story continues**

INTRODUCTION

After being reunited with his lost son Joseph, Jacob spends the last years of his life in Egypt. When the time comes for him to die, he gives his sons his deathbed blessings. As we saw earlier in the case of Isaac, children and grandchildren attached great importance to these blessings. They believed that they expressed their future destinies. Indeed, Jacob says to his sons, "Gather around so I can tell you what will happen to you in days to come."

It was specifically by describing a person's *character* that these blessings were able to predict what would happen to them, good or bad, if they continued in their ways.

Jacob begins by speaking with Joseph privately. He personally adopts Joseph's two sons and blesses them. Then he meets with all of his sons and blesses them. In many cases Jacob offers brief general blessings using vivid natural imagery, or by making plays on their names. (For example, the name "Dan" comes from the word "to judge," and so he says, "Dan will provide justice for his people.")

But in several cases Jacob addresses his sons at greater length, based on how they've lived and how they've treated him and one another. Judah and

Joseph receive lengthy blessings, while the three oldest sons, Reuben, Simeon, and Levi, are cursed.

READING

Have five people act out the scene where Jacob blesses Ephraim and Manasseh (beginning "Jacob lived in Egypt seventeen years" and ending "And to you I give one more ridge of land than to your brothers, the ridge I took from the Amorites with my sword and my bow.")

Narrator

Jacob

Joseph

Ephraim

Manasseh

The actors should use their Bibles as "scripts" and dramatize the scene for the rest of the group. (For example, have Jacob "lie in bed" and sit up when Joseph enters, have Joseph bring his sons forward and have Jacob cross his hands as he places them on their heads, etc.)

Then have group members take turns reading Jacob's deathbed blessing, or cursing, of his twelve sons. ("Then Jacob called for his sons . . .") Have one person read the opening and conclusion, and have the other members take turns reading what's said about each of the sons.

(The separate addresses to the sons begin with their names, for example, "Reuben . . .," "Simeon and Levi . . .," etc. The passage ends, "and this is what their father said to them when he blessed them, giving each the blessing appropriate to him.")

DISCUSSION

1 As Jacob prepares to bless Joseph's two sons, he reviews the covenant promises God made to him at Luz (Bethel). Throughout Genesis, we've seen how God's purposes to bring blessing to the whole world by making a covenant with Abraham, Isaac, and Jacob have advanced through unlikely agents and means. This shows that God is truly at work, and that what's happening isn't simply the outcome of earthly power arrangements.

One recurring means has been the choice of younger brothers over the firstborn: Isaac over Ishmael; Jacob over Esau; Judah and Joseph over Reuben (more about this shortly). Now the pattern extends to a fourth generation as Jacob puts Ephraim ahead of Manasseh. Jacob can't even see what he's doing, but somehow he "knows" enough to cross his hands so that his right hand rests on Ephraim's head. This prophetic (beyond human knowing) action is like the LORD's announcement to Rebekah before Esau and Jacob were even born: "the older will serve the younger."

⮑ As a group, think back over the book of Genesis and identify as many examples as you can of God's purposes being advanced through unlikely or unexpected agents or means. (Some examples are listed in the note at the end of this session. Once you've made your own list you can compare it with that one.)

⮑ Where in your own experience have you seen God advancing his purposes through unlikely or unexpected agents or means?

2 By adopting Ephraim and Manasseh as his own sons, Jacob is effectively giving Joseph's descendants a "double portion" within the nation of Israel. Joseph's descendants will be considered two tribes, not one, and they'll be given twice as much land as they would have had otherwise. (Ordinarily the firstborn son was given a "double portion" of the family property when the father died so he'd have the resources to maintain the family homestead.) Thus Jacob, clever right to the end, finds an ingenious way to give Joseph at least one of the prerogatives of the firstborn.

Nevertheless, one of the most important firstborn blessings—family supremacy—goes to Judah. Jacob tells him, "your father's sons will bow down to you." Thus both Judah and Joseph receive something of a firstborn blessing from Jacob. This may be the final expression of his ingenuity: He finds a way to let two sons share a privilege that only one should be able to have.

⊃ (Let group members do this exercise by themselves and then share their responses with the rest of the group if they'd like.) Follow Jacob's lead and write a firstborn blessing for more than one child:

If you have children of your own, write out a "firstborn blessing" for each one of them, drawing on the themes of the blessings that Jacob, Judah, and Joseph receive in Genesis (prosperity, authority, advancement, protection, God's presence).

If you don't have children, write blessings for other family members, such as your brothers and sisters or nieces and nephews, or for people who are like family to you.

NOTE

Question 1: God chooses Abraham and Sarah, a couple who couldn't have children, and who are past the childbearing years, to be the ancestors of a "great nation." Isaac and Rebekah also can't have children at first, but the covenant line continues through them. Leah, the sister Jacob didn't want to marry, becomes the mother of six of his twelve sons. Rachel, who couldn't have children at first, becomes the mother of Joseph and Benjamin. Tamar, a Canaanite woman and Judah's daughter-in-law, becomes the mother of the two great clans of the tribe of Judah. Asenath, an Egyptian woman, becomes the mother of Ephraim and Manasseh, who are adopted by Jacob and become equals with the other tribal patriarchs. You may have found other examples of unlikely agents and means in the book of Genesis yourself.

THE DEATHS OF JACOB AND JOSEPH

**Book of Genesis > Account of Jacob >
Joseph Story concludes**

INTRODUCTION

The "account of Jacob" (and the whole book of Genesis) concludes with three final scenes. Jacob dies and is taken back to the land of Canaan to be buried. Joseph's brothers ask his forgiveness, and he affirms his reconciliation with them. And when Joseph is about to die himself, he predicts that God will bring all the Israelites back to Canaan, and he makes them promise to bring his bones with them and bury him there.

READING

Have different people read these three scenes out loud:

 Jacob's death and burial. ("Then he gave them these instructions: 'I am about to be gathered to my people.'")

 The renewed reconciliation between Joseph and his brothers. ("When Joseph's brothers saw that their father was dead . . .")

⭐ *Joseph's final instructions.* ("Joseph stayed in Egypt . . .")

DISCUSSION

1 Abraham went to Canaan in obedience to God's instructions. While he and his descendants lived elsewhere at times, they always felt it was essential to return to the land God promised them and to treat it as their permanent home. This expressed their loyalty to their covenant relationship with God and their faith that God would ultimately fulfill all of his promises. This is why Jacob is so insistent on being buried in Canaan.

Accompanied by an impressive retinue from Pharaoh's court, Joseph and his brothers bring his body back and bury him there. Thus, as Genesis ends, Abraham and Sarah, Isaac and Rebekah, and Jacob and Leah are all at rest in the one small part of the land that their family has come to own, the cave of Machpelah.

➲ Where would you like to be buried, or have your ashes scattered? In what ways would you like to express your spiritual beliefs and commitments through the way you're laid to rest?

2 Joseph's brothers are afraid that he's only been waiting for their father to die before taking revenge on them. Hoping to save their own lives, they formally ask his forgiveness for what they did to him. They offer to become his slaves as just punishment for selling him into slavery. They tell him their father wanted him to forgive them. And they identify themselves as "servants of the God of your father," hoping that Joseph himself still "fears God" and will show mercy on them as fellow servants.

The brothers didn't have to worry. Joseph has maintained his remarkable awareness of God's presence and activity. He now offers a mature reflection on all that happened to him: "You intended to harm me, but God intended it for good . . ." Joseph has been able to discern how in all human actions, even actions that spring from evil intentions, God finds an opportunity to fulfill his own purposes and bring about good. Joseph can see this in his own life as he looks back over it. This same principle has been at work continually throughout the book of Genesis.

⮑ Are there things that others have done to you with bad motives or harmful intentions that you've seen God work through to bring about something good? Share your story with the group if you're comfortable doing so.

3 Like his father Jacob, Joseph sees returning to the land of Canaan as an essential act of loyalty to his covenant relationship with God, even if this means being buried there after dying in Egypt. He's so confident that God will bring the people of Israel back to Canaan that when he's about to die, he makes his family swear to bury him there. He arranges for his body to be prepared "to go." Joseph thus takes specific steps in advance of God's action, based on what his faith tells him God is going to do.

⮑ Have you ever seen someone take steps of faith like the ones Joseph takes here? What did they do? How did things turn out for them? What specific step(s) can you take today in anticipation of what your faith tells you God is going to do in your life?

⮑ How has your understanding of God changed or deepened as a result of your reading and studying the book of Genesis?

(The story in Genesis has a sequel in the book of Exodus. It tells how God did "come to the aid" of the Israelites to take them out of Egypt, despite strong resistance from Pharaoh, and bring them back to the land of Canaan.)